BRITAIN AND THE WORLD

2. The Emerging Years

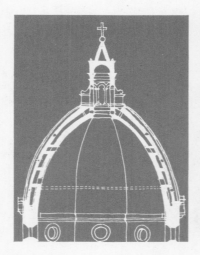
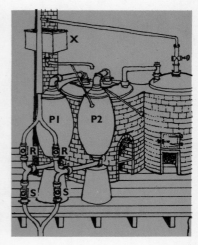

Illustrations by

TREVOR STUBLEY

0 7217 1557 5

First printed 1971
by C. Tinling & Co. Ltd,
Prescot

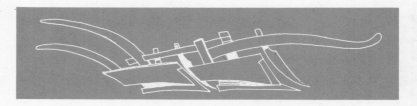

BRITAIN AND THE WORLD

The Emerging Years

By P. A. Darvill B.A., M.Litt. & W. R. Stirling M.A. (Cantab.)

SCHOFIELD & SIMS LTD · HUDDERSFIELD

PREFACE

Each of the first four books in this series is divided into two parts: a chronological narrative and a collection of ten sections. The narrative aims to preserve the flow of history, whilst the sections give details of ten basic aspects of the life of mankind.

The narrative of each book is cross-referenced with the sections by a number of marginal notes. Thus a pupil can follow up in more detail many of the topics dealt with in the narrative.

With a collection of all four volumes to hand, a teacher has, apart from the narrative, a set of ten sections covering the span of time from prehistory to the twentieth century. Such a collection can form a good starting point for project work on topics such as farming, building or a particular industry. Each set of sections is a book within a series, whilst each section is a book within a book.

ACKNOWLEDGEMENTS

The authors and publishers wish to thank the following for permission to use copyright photographs:

National Portrait Gallery: pp. 8, 14, 18 (3), 24, 25, 28, 31, 36, 37, 48, 55, 57, 58, 71, 78, 80, 84, 88, 91, 92, 94, 96, 99, 100, 102.
Radio Times Hulton Picture Library: pp. 13, 18 (3), 35, 40, 59, 62, 74, 95, 138, 146.
Ashmolean Museum: p. 14.
The Mansell Collection: pp. 17, 20, 29, 50, 70, 104, 113, 153, 154, 155 (2), 156, 156/7, 158, 159 (2), 160 (2), 164, 169, 171.
The Marquess of Exeter: p. 20. No. 190, Burghley Collection.
Lutherhalle, Lutherstadt Wittenberg: p. 21.
Lord St. Oswald's Nostell Priory Collection: p. 22.
The Trustees of the British Museum: pp. 24, 26, 45, 49, 54, 61, 69, 74, 81, 82/3, 84, 91, 142, 166, 172.
National Gallery of Ireland: p. 35.
Scottish National Portrait Gallery: p. 38.
Controller of H.M. Stationery Office: p. 50 (Crown Copyright) [SP 14/216 No. 2.].
The Curators of The Bodleian Library: p. 60.
Department of the Environment: p. 68 (Crown Copyright).
Magdalene College, Cambridge: p. 81.
Bibliothèque Nationale, Paris: pp. 86, 161.
Popperfoto: pp. 87, 100, 147.
Pitkin Pictorials Ltd. ©: p. 104.
Aerofilms Ltd.: p. 109.
A. F. Kersting: pp. 115, 116, 117.
The National Monuments Record: pp. 116, 147.
Edward J. Farmer: p. 117.
The Trustees of The National Gallery, London: p. 120.
National Maritime Museum, Greenwich: p. 127.
Science Museum, London: p. 134.
The Winchester Repeating Arms Co., Washington D.C.: p. 145.
St. Faith's Church, Gaywood, King's Lynn: p. 150.
James Philip Gray Collection of Paintings, Museum of Fine Arts, Springfield, Mass.: p. 155.
The National Museum, Cracow: p. 157.
Royal Library, Windsor Castle: pp. 157, 158.
Gallerie Gestione della Cassa di Soccorso, Florence: p. 160.
Bayerische Staatsbibliothek, München: p. 162.
Clerk of the Records, House of Lords: p. 168.
The Museum of the History of Science, Oxford: p. 174.

CONTENTS

The Narrative

The Sections

The Tudor and Stuart family tree

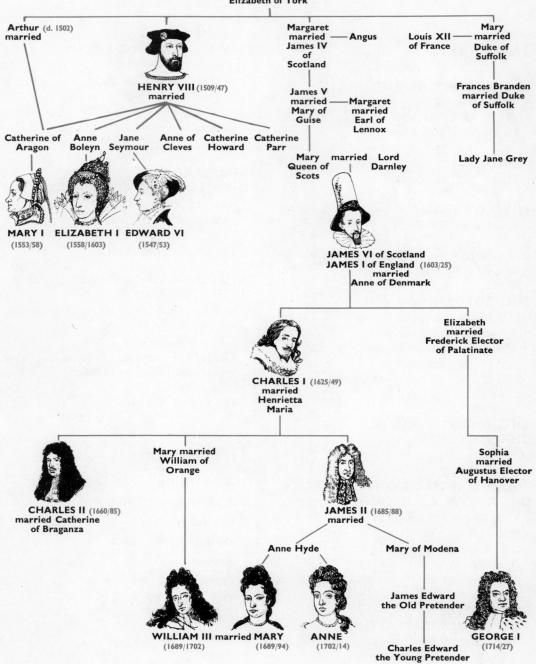

HENRY VII (1485/1509)
married
Elizabeth of York

Arthur (d. 1502)
married

HENRY VIII (1509/47)
married

Margaret
married
James IV
of
Scotland — Angus

Louis XII
of France

Mary
married
Duke of
Suffolk

James V
married
Mary of
Guise — Margaret
married
Earl of
Lennox

Frances Branden
married Duke
of Suffolk

Catherine of
Aragon
Anne
Boleyn
Jane
Seymour
Anne of
Cleves
Catherine
Howard
Catherine
Parr

Mary
Queen of
Scots   married   Lord
Darnley

Lady Jane Grey

MARY I
(1553/58)
ELIZABETH I
(1558/1603)
EDWARD VI
(1547/53)

JAMES VI of Scotland
JAMES I of England (1603/25)
married
Anne of Denmark

Elizabeth
married
Frederick Elector
of Palatinate

CHARLES I (1625/49)
married
Henrietta
Maria

Mary married
William of
Orange

Sophia
married
Augustus Elector
of Hanover

CHARLES II (1660/85)
married Catherine
of Braganza

JAMES II (1685/88)
married

Anne Hyde

Mary of Modena

James Edward
the Old Pretender

GEORGE I
(1714/27)

WILLIAM III married MARY
(1689/1702)   (1689/94)

ANNE
(1702/14)

Charles Edward
the Young Pretender

The Tudors and Stuarts

The age of the Tudors and Stuarts had almost everything—except an English king. It opened with a Welshman, Henry Tudor. A Scotsman, James Stuart, opened the next dynasty which faded away with a Dutchman, William III, and was buried by a German, George I.

Periods in history are only a convenient way of breaking down the ages into manageable units and the Tudor period is quite different from that of the Stuarts. There is a case for joining them both together, however, for from 1485 to 1714 we can see broad patterns of change taking place. When Henry VII seized the crown on Bosworth Field, England and Wales formed a small kingdom tucked away in N.W. Europe. By the time of George I the United Kingdom of England, Wales, Ireland and Scotland was the centre of a growing Empire, with ships sailing to the Americas, Africa, the Indies and to China—lands either unknown or so remote as to be almost legends two hundred and fifty years before. New kingdoms, like Holland, were born and old ones, like France, were re-born. The Renaissance of the late fifteenth century changed men's ideas about themselves and their surroundings.

The Art of War

Enter
the Tudors

Henry VII

HENRY VII (1485–1509)

Holbein's portrait of the new king shows you a very ordinary face, neither handsome nor plain, but behind the calculating eyes lay a shrewd brain. Henry was the successful Lancastrian adventurer but he knew that his title was weak and a glance at the family tree will show you who his Yorkist rivals were.

Elizabeth of York he dealt with by marrying and made sure that any sons he might have would have a legitimate claim to the throne.

Lambert Simnel and Perkin Warbeck were young men who were not important in themselves but were dangerous to Henry because of their powerful backing. Lambert, an Oxford youth, impersonated the imprisoned Earl of Warwick, and ten years later Perkin pretended to be Richard of York, one of the princes in the Tower. They were both supported by Margaret of Burgundy, the sister of Edward IV, and by the Earl of Kildare, the Lord Deputy of Ireland. Perkin even had the backing of the King of France, Charles VIII; the King of Scotland, James IV; and the Emperor Maximilian. It made no difference, however, for Henry defeated them both.

Lambert's army was shattered at Stoke in 1486. Henry spared his life but made him a kitchen scullion and had him wait upon the very men who had plotted to make him king. He ended his days a trusted falconer.

Perkin's invasion attempts were more varied but no more successful. He tried to land at Deal in Kent but Henry's supporters were waiting for him and he beat a hasty retreat. He made his base in Ireland, then in Scotland and finally he landed in Cornwall in 1497. The timing was all wrong. The men of Cornwall had already marched to London and had been defeated. They remustered and he led them against

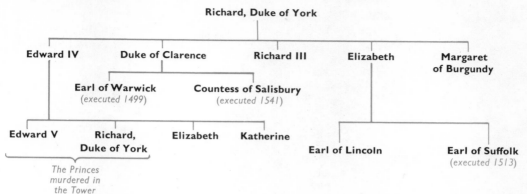

Exeter, only to be repulsed by a shower of stones. They tried again at Taunton but Perkin deserted and fled to Beaulieu Abbey. Henry did not want to make a martyr of him and was content to imprison him for two years until 1499 when further plots made Henry execute both Perkin and the Earl of Warwick.

It would be wrong to think that an overwhelming force of Yeomen of the Guard or "Beefeaters" had kept Henry's throne—the Yeomen were little more than Court Guards and there was no standing army. Henry's wits and favourable circumstances came to his aid. The Wars of the Roses had destroyed much of the strength of the barons. The common people were tired of war and the trading middle classes, particularly of London, welcomed peace and prosperity. Henry's so-called "avarice" or meanness was as important as his pikes and his new-fangled cannon, for a wealthy king and a rich middle class made a good alliance.

Henry used the lawyers, the merchants of the middle class and the lesser gentry in his parliaments to pass favourable laws, such as the Statute of Liveries of 1487 which forbade the keeping of retainers or private armies. Laws are no good unless they can be enforced, and the ordinary courts could not be relied upon to support the King against a powerful lord in his own locality. In order to give his will force, Henry used the Court of the Star Chamber and the Court of Requests, and similar courts in various parts of the country. The justice was often rough and ready, but it was quick and it seemed to offer the ordinary man a chance against local tyrants. The Tudors liked to make the punishment fit the crime, as in the reign of Elizabeth when a man who had beaten his grandfather was ordered to be whipped in front of a picture of the old gentleman. Sometimes they were designed to make the offender look

A Yeoman of the Guard

Government

9

silly, as in the reign of Henry VIII when John Tyndal was sentenced to ride with his face to the horse's tail, having papers on his head and the New Testament pinned to his clothing. His crime? Distributing copies of the New Testament.

How Henry VII attacked his Overmighty Subjects

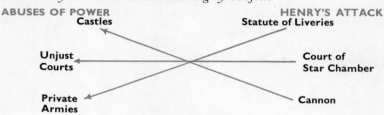

ABUSES OF POWER	HENRY'S ATTACK
Castles	Statute of Liveries
Unjust Courts	Court of Star Chamber
Private Armies	Cannon

The Court frequently exacted heavy fines, for it was Henry's policy to weaken his "overmighty subjects" and to fill his own pockets. Sir Francis Bacon said, "The less blood he drew, the more he took of treasure"—sometimes a fine might be as high as £30,000—one wonders if he ever managed to collect it.

A rich king has a better chance of being successful than a poor one. All the Tudors and Stuarts knew this, but none of them could manage to get full control of money matters. We shall see that the Stuarts paid dearly when they tried, but Henry VII came nearest to success. He increased the income of his Exchequer threefold, and he left a full Treasury to his son. People do not like to pay taxes in any age and Tudor people were no exception. Henry's tax collectors, Empson and Dudley or "the ravening wolves", as they were called, grew to be hated. The myth of Cardinal Morton's "fork" shows how disliked Henry's money-raising ventures were. The story goes that if Morton visited a rich man he extracted a forced loan on the plea that the man was rich and could afford it. If he visited a poor noble he still got his "loan", arguing that the man must have his money hidden away. What is true is that Henry would sell important positions, charge high fees in the courts, sell pardons and fine heavily. In 1504 he even raised a tax to pay for the knighthood of his son Arthur, who had died fourteen years earlier!—but these events came later in his reign when he was becoming a Scrooge.

He also used sensible means of raising money—by the wise administration of the Crown lands and the collection of customs duties. He encouraged trade, especially the wool trade, and the trade treaty of 1496, called the Magnus Intercursus, gave English merchants good trading terms in Flanders, where most of their wool went. He encouraged traders to challenge the foreign control of English trade. Companies such as the

A merchant of the sixteenth century

Industry and Trade

Map of the world according to Behaim, 1492

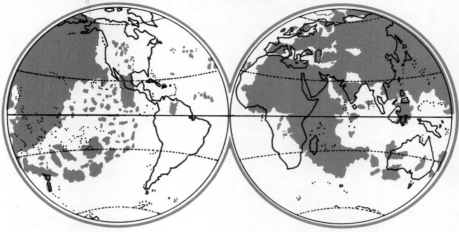

German Hanseatic League with its headquarters at the Steel-yard where Paddington Station stands now, had control of trade with the Baltic. Henry helped the English Merchant Adventurers to break into this rich trade. Had Henry been more adventuresome, he might have done more to increase England's wealth by encouraging the sailors who were seeking new ways to the East across the Atlantic, and who were discovering the New World of the Americas in the process. In the mid-fifteenth century Portugal, under their *Prince Henry the Navigator*, had pioneered the ocean routes to India round the coast of Africa. *Bartholomew Diaz* had accidentally discovered the route round the Cape of Good Hope in 1487–88, and *Vasco da Gama* had

Transport by Sea

Map of the world according to Homan, 1716

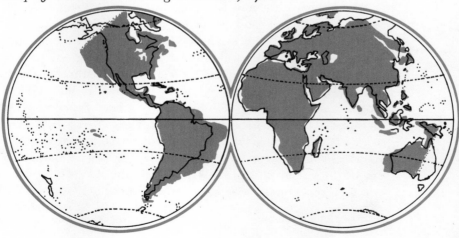

11

The Santa Maria

eventually reached Calicut in India in 1497. *Christopher Colombus* had discovered the Bahamas and Cuba in 1492 when he was in the service of Spain, but he had earlier hawked his project at the Court of Henry VII only to be refused by the cautious monarch. England, therefore, played second fiddle to Spain in the Americas and to Portugal in the Indies for some time to come. Henry had been impressed by *John Cabot*, a Genoese settled in Bristol, and allowed him to sail from this port in 1497 heading for the Americas. John reached "Newfoundland" and Nova Scotia, which he thought was part of the Chinese Empire. He opened up the northern part of America for future English settlement. Henry, true to form, gave him £10 for his pains. John Cabot's son, Sebastian, carried on the family tradition of exploring the coast of North America under Henry VIII, who again was not particularly interested in exploration. England's colonial greatness in the next centuries owes very little to the early Tudor kings. Henry VII died a rich man and, unlike later monarchs, he had not gone cap in hand to Parliament to get his wealth.

Wars are a great expense and Henry preferred to win by diplomacy. He did have a three-weeks' war with France in 1491. He made a profit from the war levies granted by Parliament and from the 745 000 gold crowns "pay-off" from Charles VIII, who was anxious to get rid of the troublesome English.

Princes and princesses have been pawns in diplomacy for centuries and Henry knew the rules of the game. He arranged a marriage between his eldest son, Arthur, and Catherine of Aragon, and gained both the friendship of Ferdinand and Isabella of Spain and a handsome dowry. When Arthur died at the early age of 14, Henry betrothed his second son, Henry, to the young widow and he even tried to get a second dowry out of Ferdinand and Isabella. Margaret, his daughter, married James IV of Scotland and paved the way for the day when the Stuarts would rule England. These foreign marriages were useful, too, in stopping the claims to the throne which might arise if royal children married English nobles. Henry took a shaky throne in 1485, but he left it one of the strongest in Europe. He was lucky that the "powers" in Europe were so busy watching each other that they allowed him to strengthen England without interference, and Henry was wise enough to use his luck. Bacon said of Henry VII—he was "one of the best sorts of wonders, a wonder for wise men."

"King Hal"

HENRY VIII (1509—47)

Henry VIII was not quite eighteen when he succeeded to his father's throne. Thanks to the painstaking reign of Henry VII he inherited a full treasury and a secure right to his crown, for with a Lancastrian father and a Yorkist mother, the fear of another "War of the Roses" was gone for ever—or was it?

A greater contrast than the two Henrys would be hard to find. His portraits show Henry VIII as a robust figure of a man, good at all manly pastimes, a follower of the hunt, a tennis player, and a wrestler to be reckoned with. This handsome prince had intelligence. He was a patron of the arts and a lively wit. There were also darker sides to his character. His pleasures were not simple, they needed money, lots of it, and even the hoards of Henry VII were insufficient to meet his extravagance. There was ruthlessness there too, and one of his first acts was to execute his father's tax collectors, Empson and Dudley, on a trumped-up charge of treason in order to please popular fancy. Many more were to follow them to Tower Hill if Henry felt it was right.

The opening years of his reign pleased his people and caught the imagination of Europe. He fulfilled his father's wish and within six months had married his brother's widow, Catherine of Aragon, although he needed the special permission of the Pope to do so. Spain and England were allies and Henry's wish for personal glory was encouraged by his father-in-law, Ferdinand. France was the traditional scene for an English show of arms. In 1512 England joined Spain, Venice and the Papacy and invaded France. After a disastrous start, Henry led his army personally and in 1513 routed the French at the Battle of Spurs. The Scots took the opportunity whilst Henry was in France to invade England but they were defeated at Flodden. Meanwhile, Ferdinand had retired from the war

Henry VIII (aged twenty)

The Art of War

13

and an angry and wiser Henry made his peace with France in 1514, and renounced any ideas of conquering France. During the next fifteen years the spotlight was not upon Henry but upon his chief minister, Thomas Wolsey, for Henry was too busy with the thrills of the chase to be bothered by the dreary business of government. This was a state of affairs well liked by the ambitious Wolsey.

Thomas Wolsey was the son of an Ipswich innkeeper and butcher. He took his degree at Oxford at the age of fifteen and like many more of less than noble birth, he saw that his best chance lay in the Church. His ordinary background and his ambition made him just the sort of man the Tudors liked to use. "Use" is the right word, for however high Wolsey appeared to fly he soared not one inch higher than the King wished him to and he plunged to earth the moment he had outlived his usefulness.

Hampton Court was built by Thomas Wolsey. It was big, grand and rivalled the royal palaces of Westminster and Eltham. It showed how important the Ipswich boy had become, and how much wealth and power he enjoyed. By 1518 Wolsey was leader of the Church and leader of the State— beginning as Dean of Lincoln in 1509, Bishop of Tournai in France in 1513, Bishop of Lincoln, then Archbishop of York in

Cardinal Wolsey

Hampton Court Palace in 1538

Ashmolean Museum,

1514, not to mention the bishoprics of Bath and Wells and later Durham and Winchester. The Pope made him a Cardinal in 1515 and Papal Legate in 1518. Only the Archbishopric of Canterbury escaped him for the aged Warham refused to die; even so, Wolsey was supreme in the Church. A person who holds so many positions in the Church is called a "pluralist", and though he visited few of these places he drew his income from all of them. Although he was not a monk he became Abbot of St Albans in order to enjoy its income. There is something wrong in a Church when a man can use holy offices for personal gain and Cardinal Wolsey's corruption showed the need for a reformed Church. He was a man of great intelligence and energy and he knew how to handle the King. This is why he was made Lord Chancellor in 1515 and hence the greatest man in all England next to the King.

A beggar

Building

What did he do with all his power? Apart from the monuments of Hampton Court and Christ Church College at Oxford which he founded, it is difficult to see what else he did which was lasting. To his credit he used the Court of the Star Chamber and the Court of Chancery to cut through legal red tape and he tried to bring justice to rich and poor alike. The poor blessed him for it, but many nobles and jealous lawyers hated him.

Government

Wolsey did not understand finance. One cannot blame him for failing to realise that great changes were afoot which were destroying the old England of manor and open field. These changes took another 250 years to work themselves out. The population was increasing, prices were rising and more and more beggars, both real and "sturdy", tried to wheedle or extort a "groat or an angel" from fearful passers-by. People at the time, including Wolsey, tried to blame it all on sheep and enclosures but he could do nothing to stop bread costing more money. He could not hide the fact that the royal coffers, so full in 1509, were now empty and like Tudor and Stuart after him he could not persuade an unwilling Parliament to foot the bill of day-to-day government, let alone royal extravagances. In 1524, he tried to raise an Amicable Grant and nearly caused rebellions in East Anglia and Kent. Henry had to step in himself to save the day.

Agriculture

Even in the field of foreign affairs, where Wolsey is supposed to have shone, all his efforts were in vain. It is quite wrong to suppose that he invented the so-called "balance of power" whereby a third party holds the balance between two others. In this case England held it between Francis I of France and Charles V of Spain and the Holy Roman Empire.

An angel and a half-groat

NORWAY
SWEDEN
SCOTLAND

Boundary of the H
Roman Empire

Dominions of the
House of Hapsburg

Brandenburg

Lands of the
Union of Calmar

Church lands

NORTH SEA

IRELAND

WALES

ENGLAND

London

Copenhagen

PRUSSIA

HOLSTEIN

POMERANIA

Hamburg

BRANDENBURG

Warsaw

Antwerp

HESSE

Cologne

Elbe

LUSATIA

SILESIA

Oder

POLAND

NETHERLANDS

SAXONY

BRITTANY

LUXEMBURG

Paris

LOWER

UPPER
PALATINATE

PALATINATE

BOHEMIA

MORAVIA

ATLANTIC OCEAN

Rhine

LORRAINE

Seine

FRANCHE

Loire

COMTE

FRANCE

BRESSE
BUGEY

SWISS

CONFEDERATION

AUSTRIA

Munich

Vienna

STYRIA

TYROL

CARINTHIA

HUNGARY

SAVOY

Milan

Venice

Danube

Garonne

Rhône

Po

Genoa

Florence

PAPAL

ADRIATIC SEA

Constantinop

PORTUGAL

SPAIN

Madrid

Ebro

ARAGON

STATES

Rome

OTTOMAN EMPIRE

Lisbon

CASTILE

Guadalquivir

Naples

NAPLES

MEDITERRANEAN SEA

SICILY

Europe and the Balance of Power 1519

A longbowman

A glance at the map will show you that from 1519, when Charles V succeeded his grandfather as Holy Roman Emperor, there were really only two great powers in Europe—the Hapsburg lands, Austria and Spain, and France. The struggles which followed are far more personal than national and you must not think of Europe as being divided into nations as it is today. Nations were emerging—France, Spain, England and Holland—but they were still bundles of loyalties to a dominant king rather than the nations we know. Henry, Francis and Charles were "despots", ruling by their own will. They were wilful and young and all Europe was their arena. England was not as important as the other two powers. It is true that both Charles and Francis sought the friendship of Henry and that England might appear to hold a balance. Wolsey fancied himself, too, as "the arbiter of Christendom" and lived up to this role of "go-between".

16

He wanted above all else to be made Pope and used England's foreign policy to try to achieve this end. Foreign policy is not the whim of one man but is shaped by many forces, not least of these is trade. In the sixteenth century the wool trade was of particular importance. Charles V controlled Flanders, the largest market for English wool. An alliance with Charles was an obvious choice, even if this did upset any balance which might exist, for Charles's resources were greater than those of Francis, and furthermore his lands surrounded France. He was only too pleased to hint that he would help Wolsey to become Pope, and to promise to rid Italy of the pestilent French and free the Pope from their threat.

What followed shows how sly diplomacy was—for Henry met Francis in great splendour just outside Calais with tournaments, feasting and display. It was known as the Field of the Cloth of Gold. Later, at a quiet meeting with Charles at Gravelines, the English-Hapsburg alliance was arranged (1521). In fact, nothing came of these meetings and England got nothing for her pains. Pope Leo X died in 1521, but Wolsey did not succeed him. The new Pope feared Charles's success and made peace with Francis. English armies fared badly in France and Wolsey followed the Pope and pulled out of the war. Charles went from strength to strength and in 1526 a mutinous Hapsburg army seized Rome and sacked it. Wolsey changed sides and in 1528 joined the Holy League, along with Francis, to free the Pope from Charles's domination. A dismal failure resulted, France was defeated, the Pope had no alternative but to make peace with Charles, and England was so unimportant that she was not even consulted about the peace. So much for Wolsey's foreign designs.

The Field of the Cloth of Gold

17

Catherine of Aragon

Anne Boleyn

Jane Seymour

Anne of Cleves

Catherine Howard

Henry VIII and wives go together: Catherine of Aragon—divorced; Anne Boleyn—beheaded; Jane Seymour—died; Anne of Cleves—divorced; Catherine Howard—beheaded; Catherine Parr—outlived him. They make quite a list, yet Henry did not marry merely to change his loves. Royal marriages had little to do with romance, they were business. Henry had fallen in love with Anne Boleyn it is true, but his roving eye had lighted up at a pretty face before and was to do so again. The King's desire to get rid of Catherine of Aragon was a queer mixture of royal interests. In part it was religious conscience, but it was also a matter of national security for a male heir was needed to make sure the Tudors stayed on the throne. Henry was convinced that the death of five children in infancy—only Mary survived—was a sign of God's displeasure at his marriage with his brother's widow. You will recall that he had needed the Pope's special permission to marry. He wanted a legitimate son and so the wheels of the "Great Divorce" were set in motion. Wolsey knew that he must get the King his way or he would fall. All depended upon the success of the Holy League—for a free Pope might well give Henry his way and annul his marriage. Had Henry not supported the Pope in war against both Francis and Charles? Had Henry not even written a volume against the heretic Luther, and earned the title Fidei Defensor; the F.D. we see on British coins to this day? The failure of the League meant a Pope tied to Charles V. Charles was the nephew of Catherine of Aragon and he would never agree to the divorce.

Cardinals Campeggio and Wolsey were appointed to deal with the case, Campeggio being under secret instructions from Rome. He delayed and delayed in order to see how the war in Italy would swing, but eventually the case was heard at

18

Catherine Parr

Blackfriars in 1529. Queen Catherine is the one figure who emerges with honour. Henry tried every trick in the book to prove his marriage wrong and the Pope's servants suggested every possible alternative, in order to avoid an open clash. They even suggested that Catherine should retire to a nunnery. The victory of Charles at Cambrai sealed the matter. The divorce case was recalled to Rome a week before the official peace treaty. Henry stripped Wolsey of all his offices except Archbishop of York, and within twelve months he was called to London on a charge of high treason. He never answered the charge for he died on his way at Leicester Abbey. "Would that I had served my God as well as I had served my King" were supposed to have been his last words. It would have been more appropriate if he had said, "Would that I had served my God as well as I have tried to serve myself."

The Rise and Fall of Wolsey

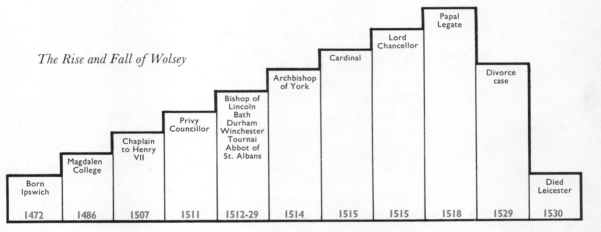

Born Ipswich	Magdalen College	Chaplain to Henry VII	Privy Councillor	Bishop of Lincoln Bath Durham Winchester Tournai Abbot of St. Albans	Archbishop of York	Cardinal	Lord Chancellor	Papal Legate	Divorce case	Died Leicester
1472	1486	1507	1511	1512-29	1514	1515	1515	1518	1529	1530

Henry still hoped that the Pope would grant a divorce. As a king, he was not a revolutionary so he now began a complicated game of fencing, using parliament as his foil and thrusting at the Roman Catholic Church in England. He hoped to force the Pope to agree to his request rather than see England lost to the Catholic cause. The Annates Act of 1532 withheld payments of church taxes to Rome. Henry could amend this if the Pope saw the light! The Pope did not. In 1533 Cranmer, the new Archbishop of Canterbury, granted Henry his divorce. Henry had married Anne secretly, anyway, some months before, but he now had her crowned in Westminster Abbey. The Act in Restraint of Appeals stopped cases being transferred from England to Rome and for the first time talks of "this realm of England is a realm governed by one Supreme Head and King". The Pope is thought of as a foreign power

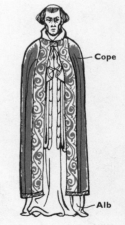

A priest in cope and alb

19

Erasmus

Ideas

Burghley Collection

Martin Luther

who was not wanted in England. "The Bishop of Rome treadeth under foot God's laws and the King's," were Archbishop Cranmer's words—and however much Henry had hoped to avoid a break with Rome, this was now complete. The Pope had no power in England, Henry had all and was Head of the Church *in* England as well. It was only a matter of time before the Church *of* England, a Protestant Church, was born. To the end of his days Henry denied the power of the Pope, but insisted England was Catholic. The Act of Six Articles in 1539 and the King's Book of 1543 both proclaimed that the English Church was truly Catholic. Some men, however, had supported Henry's quarrel from religious convictions and they would not be content with a compromise.

Henry's break with Rome is part of a European movement against the Roman Catholic Church. Good churchmen, like *Erasmus* in Flanders, were dissatisfied with the Church. His book, *The Praise of Folly*, poked fun at the corruption in the Church. There were other sincere religious people who wanted a more vigorous attack on the Church. Martin Luther and John Calvin were two such people and their protests have given us the name "Protestantism"; their desire to reform the Church is known as the "Reformation".

In order to understand where Henry's quarrel with the Pope fits into the history of the Reformation elsewhere, we should take a look at two of the people most concerned with the changes in Europe. *Martin Luther* was the son of a Saxon miner, who became a monk and a lecturer at the University of Wittenberg. He was a man of violent and deep moods, very much concerned with a sense of sin. He grew to disagree with the Church's teaching that it could forgive sins and that it could waive the usual signs of penitence, such as pilgrimages, by the payment of "indulgences". When Martin Tetzel, a Dominican friar, travelled through Germany selling such indulgences, Luther's anger exploded and he listed ninety-five reasons, or theses, why the Pope should not do this and had it pinned to the Church door at Wittenberg. He followed this up by a more sweeping condemnation of the "wrongs" of the Church and the Pope threatened to excommunicate him, that is, to refuse him the services and sacraments of the Church. Luther challenged the Pope's right by having the Papal Bull burnt publicly. In 1521 he was called to a Diet, a meeting of the German princes at Worms and was ordered to recant. Luther's reply: "Here I stand. I cannot do otherwise", is one of the famous quotes of history and showed Luther's courage and obstinacy. His protest was the origin of the word "Protestant".

20

Luther preaching

He knew, however, that he had the backing of the powerful Elector of Saxony and other German princes who were happy to break from the Pope for reasons similar to those of Henry VIII. Luther was outlawed by the Diet and was protected at Wartburg by the Elector of Saxony. It was during this time that he translated the New Testament into German so that the "Word of God" could be read by everyone. The effect was similar to that of the English Bible introduced during Henry VIII's reign. The Reformation replaced the authority of the Pope by the authority of the open Bible and the authority of princes. The princes for reasons good and bad took sides—for Luther and against—and eventually civil war broke out. Many crimes against humanity are committed in the name of religion.

John Calvin was French, born at Noyon, and was a lawyer not a priest. The teachings of Luther and other reformers had spread into France, where the Protestants were known as Huguenots. By 1535 Calvin was one of them and had written his famous "Institutes"—a careful account of the new teachings. It was in the Swiss city of Geneva that he was invited to put his teachings into practice and to create a city of God. Calvinist rule was harsh and unyielding and he was driven from Geneva for a while. Most reformers believe in the absolute rightness of their cause and this results in intolerance of other faiths. Calvin's teaching had a great influence in Britain, particularly in Scotland, where John Knox founded the Presbyterian Church. In England, Calvin's followers became known as Puritans, who were very much a force in the land during the seventeenth century.

John Calvin

21

Sir Thomas More and his family

In the year Calvin was writing his "Institutes", the "Supreme Head of the Church in England", Henry VIII, was busy using his supremacy to get rid of all opposition. He had already executed two saintly Roman Catholics, Cardinal Fisher and Sir Thomas More, who refused to accept Henry as head of the Church. More had been Henry's friend and he was universally respected, but Henry valued obedience before love and the path to Tower Hill was already becoming well worn. Despite his excesses and the sheer cheek of his break with the Pope, Henry got his own way, for he had the support of the people who mattered. Some people supported him for religious reasons, some for self-seeking reasons, and others for money and the "pickings" which they hoped to get from the carcase of the Church.

The Roman Catholic Church had been the greatest single landowner in the country. Henry's treasury was empty and the monasteries were rich, even though they had been founded on poverty, chastity and obedience. What more natural than that the King should relieve them of their wealth? Thomas Cromwell, Henry's right-hand man since Wolsey, was the genius behind most of the Acts of the Reformation Parliament, and when he was made Vicar-General in 1535 he was the ideal "fault-finder". He despatched visitors to look into the condition of the monasteries, who saw and recorded those things which would serve the King's cause. Their findings, true in many details, were nevertheless hypocrisy and humbug. If the Bishop of Lincoln could write in the fifteenth century, a hundred years before the Dissolution of the Monasteries, of the monasteries at Huntingdon and St Neots, "There is nothing else here but drunkenness and surfeit, disobedience and contempt . . . sloth and every other thing which is on the downward path to evil and drags a man to hell," you can guess what lurid faults Cromwell's visitors found.

In 1536, 376 smaller monasteries whose income was less than £200 a year were closed, their lands and income confiscated. Three years later the bigger ones went the same way. The ruins of Fountains Abbey in Yorkshire, or Tintern Abbey in the Wye Valley are monuments to the success of these attacks. Most of the lands were sold to willing landowners who now had a money stake in the Reformation. The sale money and incomes went into the bottomless pit of Henry's treasury. He founded a few schools, created six new bishoprics and five professorships at universities, but these were nothing compared to the wealth which was seized. Henry got away with it—but only just, for Lincolnshire rose in rebellion in 1536 and Yorkshire followed, led by Robert Aske. The rebellion was caused by things other than religion. But for Aske, at least, religion was the main reason. Henry had no standing army and appeared to be in a serious situation for, despite the failure of the Lincolnshire rising, the Pilgrimage of Grace went from strength to strength. At one time, 30 000 men were under arms in Doncaster. The Duke of Norfolk acted as Henry's representative and between them they promised the earth to the angry Yorkshiremen, for example that the Pope's authority should be restored and that Parliament should be reformed. Aske persuaded the rebels to go home in the December and although there were odd risings in 1537, Henry had first divided and then conquered his enemies. He broke every promise he had made. Aske and some 220 to 250 other

Tintern Abbey

Title page from the Great Bible 1539

*Agriculture
Government*

A late portrait of Henry VIII

minor leaders were executed and the Pilgrimage was tricked to defeat. The ruthless way it was stamped out prevented further opposition.

So much for the upheavals of Henry's reign. Luther summed him up nicely when he said: "Junker Harry meant to be God and to do as pleased himself."

Anne Boleyn provided him with another daughter, Elizabeth, as unwanted as Catherine of Aragon's Mary, but in 1537 Jane Seymour gave him his long hoped for son and heir, Edward. Jane died but Edward survived, although he was a weak child. The Tudor throne seemed safe once again. But Henry rampaged to the end. In 1540 the faithful Cromwell fell out of favour as had Wolsey and More, and was executed. It was as dangerous to be Henry's friend as his enemy. Henry's figure might have got bulkier and his jowl looser, but his ambitions did not lessen with middle age. He proclaimed himself King of Ireland and, turning his attention to Scotland, tried, like other English kings before him, to bring the canny Scots to heel. In 1542 James V of Scotland was defeated at Solway Moss in one of the cheapest battles in history—the English lost seven men, the Scots twenty, but the rest were in full flight and James died broken-hearted. The infant Mary, who grew up to be the ill-fated Queen of Scots, succeeded him and was sent to France. By now England was fighting on two fronts for the Scots sought an alliance with France by the marriage of Mary to a French prince. Henry turned on France and fought an unsuccessful war, during which England was invaded in 1545 by both the Scots and the French, who landed on the Isle of Wight. In a way the reaction of the English people to these setbacks is a compliment to Henry, for with all his faults he could still capture the imagination and the loyalty of his subjects. He died in 1547, his bloated figure and character a far cry from the golden prince of 1509.

The Boy King

EDWARD VI (1547–53)

The Boy King Edward can hardly be said to have ruled for he was only nine when he became king, and not quite sixteen when he died of tuberculosis. His so-called reign can be told in the story of two men—Edward Seymour, titled Duke of Somerset and uncle to the King, and John Dudley, titled Duke of Northumberland and the son of the same Dudley who had been tax-collector in Henry VII's reign.

The Duke of Somerset, sometimes called "the good duke", was a man born before his age in his ideas of tolerance and concern for the poor, yet he suffered from his share of human frailty, too, for he was conceited, high-handed and a poor governor. He was Lord Protector and therefore the leader during the Regency; that is, a period when a king is too young to rule himself. The tolerance he preached caused Protestant reformers to pour into the country now that no "Junker Harry" was likely to give them a hot reception. Archbishop Cranmer was dismayed by the swing of the religious pendulum so far to the left and the English Prayer Book of 1549 resulted. This forerunner of our present prayer book tried to steer a middle course—images were abolished, the clergy could marry and the Communion Service allowed the wine to be taken by the lay people of the congregation. There were still those who yearned for the old ways of the Mass, however, and the West Country rose in rebellion. In the same year Norfolk rose too, under a leader called Ket. Religious causes were mixed up with cries against the enclosures for sheep, which were taking place in East Anglia. Thomas More had written two decades earlier in his book *Utopia*—"Sheep have become devourers of men . . . they unpeople villages and towns." Ket's men protested by ritually killing and eating 20 000 sheep. The risings were put down by the prompt action of local landowners led by

Edward VI

Agriculture

25

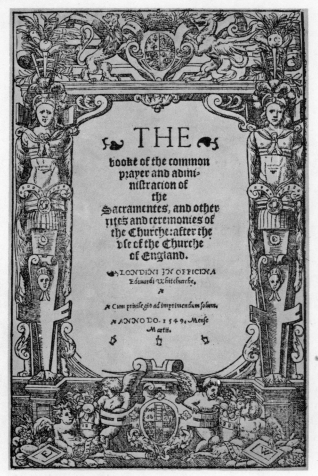

The title page from Edward VI's prayer book

Russell and Herbet in the West, and Warwick in the East. Somerset was too muddled to take any such action. He sympathised with Ket's cause, but so had Tudor ministers since 1488. An Act of Parliament in 1489 and another in 1534 tried to restrict sheep farming, but despite government efforts to enforce them they failed. Somerset had sent out commissioners a year before the rebellion to try to find out the extent to which sheep farming was replacing the growing of crops. Somerset's policy threatened the landowners' profits from wool sales and led to his downfall. Somerset was arrested by a group of Councillors in 1549 but was released by the Earl of Warwick, later Duke of Northumberland, who sought to make Somerset his puppet in the Council. When this scheme failed, he had Somerset sent to

Government

the Tower again and he was executed in 1551.

Agriculture

The Duke of Northumberland was quite different from Somerset. He was ambitious, selfish and ruthless and he ruled England in the interests of the landowning classes. Under him enclosures were welcomed, and like Henry before him, he had coins minted which were so debased that a shilling had only three-pennyworth of silver in it. Northumberland's religion was his own. He supported the Protestants because the new faith offered him more personal gain on earth than the old did in heaven. During the time he controlled the government the extreme Protestants had a field day. Not only were images banned but so were bells, and in 1552 the Second or Revised Prayer Book made quite certain that the Church of England was stripped of the last signs of Roman Catholic worship. The "Mass" had been replaced by "Communion" in 1549, now the vestments of the priests went too, even the term "priest" was replaced by "minister" and "altar" by "table". The ordinary people were bemused by all this play with words

26

and although they now had a Bible and a Service in English, it meant less to them because it was unfamiliar compared to the well-known rites of the "old Church". The new Prayer Book had hardly been introduced when the death of Edward brought a dramatic change.

Northumberland knew that his power depended on Edward's health and he took steps to keep this power at all costs. Edward was persuaded to proclaim that neither of his sisters, Mary or Elizabeth, could rule because they were illegitimate and that his true heir was *Lady Jane Grey*, the grand-daughter of Henry VIII's sister Mary. Northumberland's son, Lord Guildford Dudley, was married to Jane. The "Nine Days Queen" is one of the pitiful figures of the Tudor period. She was only seventeen but her youth and innocence could not save her. Northumberland reckoned without the temper of the people and on his way to East Anglia he was told that the Council had proclaimed Mary Queen, as befitted the daughter of Henry Tudor. His hat throwing in Cambridge market place in her favour, his plea that he had always been a true Catholic, were no use, for by the standards of his age Northumberland deserved to die. Jane's last words, written in the prayer book she carried to the block, have a ring of sincerity and faith which a Northumberland could never understand—"There is a time to be born and a time to die, and the day of death is better than the day of our birth. Yours as The Lord knoweth as a friend. Jane Dudley."

The execution of Lady Jane Grey

An Unhappy Monarch

Mary I

Philip II

Government

MARY I (1553–58)

Mary came to the throne with the cheers of her people ringing in her ears. She left it after five long years in a dismal silence and with the name of "Bloody Mary" written in the annals of history, yet Mary deserved neither the cheers nor the scorn. The people cheered her because she was the daughter of Henry, and they cursed her because she seemed to have betrayed her Tudor and her English heritage in favour of her Spanish blood, her Spanish husband and her Roman Catholic faith. How strange that a gentle and generous woman, with little guile, should have such a disastrous reign and breed such hate, whilst her cruel and cunning father should win such love. Mary was a misfit. She was more like the Stuarts than the Tudors. She had good intentions but could not understand the feelings of her people.

If Mary's faith had let her go back to the religious state of affairs in "good King Harry's day" the people would have been only too happy. Her determination to bring England back to the Roman Catholic faith and to the authority of the Pope, and her marriage with Philip of Spain were very unpopular. Mary married Philip in Winchester Cathedral in 1554 and although Parliament refused to crown him he was in fact King of England and England was spliced with Spain in a Hapsburg alliance—how Henry must have turned in his grave! By November 1554 Mary had called three parliaments, and this time she found one which would almost do as it was told. Cardinal Pole, an exiled English Catholic, was sent by the Pope to accept England's reconciliation with Rome—"to call us home again into the right way from whence we have all this long while wandered and strayed abroad". Many of Henry's Acts against the Roman Catholic Church were wiped away, but Parliament would not agree to give back the con-

28

The Burning of Latimer and Ridley

fiscated Church lands. It passed new heresy and treason laws
to enforce the return to the Church and Mary used them to
purge in fire all those who would not accept the "true faith".
Philip, less religious and more cautious, advised her to go
slowly but burning righteousness could only see burning as the
salvation of her country. The trials started in January 1555
and nearly 300 men and women were burnt for their faith
at Smithfield and other execution spots. The Bishops Latimer
and Ridley died at Oxford and the words of Latimer were to
be only too true—"We shall this day light such a candle by
God's grace in England as I trust shall never be put out."
Englishmen had no stomach for burning flesh and the Smithfield Fires did more for the Protestant cause than Calvin's
teachings. Cranmer, too, after recanting and trying to avoid

the stake, finally died bravely, plunging the hand which had signed the confession into the fire—"And for as much as my hand offended in writing contrary to my heart, it shall be first burned". Most of the martyrs, enshrined in Foxe's "Book of Martyrs", were ordinary folk. The burnings failed to get rid of their new faith. The Protestants were here to stay.

Mary's marriage fared no better than her religious hopes. Philip returned to Spain in 1555 and as passionately as Mary had wanted a child none had been forthcoming. Some people seem born to tragedy and Mary is a good example. Her marriage was unhappy and unpopular and through it England was dragged into her husband's wars. Calais was lost in the war with France and Mary's unpopularity increased. Ironically, England was better off without Calais for she no longer had the expense of keeping a garrison in a foreign land. Mary died a few months later—it is said with Calais engraved on her heart.

Calais

The
Golden Age
and Gloriana

ELIZABETH I (1558–1603)

Elizabeth was the daughter of Anne Boleyn and because of it was lucky to be alive in 1558, for she had nearly been executed at the beginning of Mary's reign. For a time she was imprisoned in the Tower. Once her mother had fallen from Henry's favour, Elizabeth was not in the public eye. After all an elder sister and a younger brother were likely to ascend the throne before her. During these early years she had learned to control her natural fiery temper. She did not have red hair for nothing. In many ways she was her father's daughter—gay, intelligent, self-willed, yet with almost a second sight for governing. Her personal character does not compare with Mary's for she could be fickle, underhand, untruthful, but she could and she did rule as only a true Tudor could. She had the common sense to see that whatever she did, she must do it in easy stages and not force the issue. She was not deeply religious but because she was Henry's daughter people expected her to support the Church of England. She wanted to be tolerant and it was easy in the early years of her reign for a good Catholic to remain so, but later Elizabeth would imprison and execute for "treason" not "heresy".

The Church pendulum swung back once again away from Rome. A new Act of Supremacy was passed in 1558 which made her "Supreme Governor of this realm, as well in all spiritual and ecclesiastical things or causes as temporal". This Act was given teeth by an Act of Uniformity which took Cranmer's Second Prayer Book of 1552 as its mainstay. It insisted on attendance at Church, or the payment of a shilling fine—which was an easier choice than the Smithfield Fires and even then the fines were rarely collected. She had a difficult job to get these Acts through Parliament and all but one bishop refused to take the oath of allegiance, but only some

Elizabeth I

Ideas

31

The entrance to a priest hole

A Jesuit priest

300 ordinary clergy felt strongly enough to refuse. Most people grew to accept the new Church of England, only the faithful extremes of Catholic and Calvinist detested it. After 1571 there is a different tale to tell for the Pope had grown tired of Elizabeth's broad hints that she might be persuaded to become a good Catholic and had excommunicated her, declared her a heretic and called on Catholics to overthrow "the pretender Queen of England"—"And we do command and charge all and every . . . not to obey her or her orders." Elizabeth became the target for assassination and English Catholics were torn between their religious faith and their loyalty to the Queen. Most chose to practise their faith and avoid trouble, others felt in all honesty that to overthrow Elizabeth would be an act of faith, whilst others used it as an excuse to try and get rid of her for their own ends.

The Catholic Church had been putting its own house in order and we call this reformation within the Church, the Counter-Reformation. Elizabeth's Church of England was not going to get its own way and two sets of Catholic "commandos" were trained to win back the souls of Protestants and screw up the courage of Catholics. A college was set up at Douai in France by an exiled Englishman, William Allen, to train young English Catholics to "return to England for the salvation of souls". The Jesuits, a religious order set up on military lines by Ignatius Loyola in Spain, were particularly keen and organised a battle-of-souls mission to keep their faith alive in England. They came in 1580 and were led by a brave English Catholic, Edmund Campion. They were not politicians, nor were they Spanish spies, but because politics and religion were so hopelessly mixed up, Elizabeth's government chose to lump honest priests and plotting politicians together as traitors and rooted out the Jesuits whenever they could be found. Catholic families took to hiding their visiting priests in tiny secret rooms, like the one at Towneley Hall, Burnley, and into these "priest holes" the priests would be pushed if the troopers, informed by some local busybody, thundered at the door. If they were caught they were either given a quiet trial by a local Justice of the Peace and strung from the nearest gallows, or they were hung, drawn and quartered on the infamous gibbet at Tyburn. Edmund Campion was martyred for his faith in 1581. The ordinary Englishman grew to accept the idea that "Catholic = Traitor". When Sir Francis Knollys asked Campion—"Do you renounce the Pope" and he replied "I am a Catholic", an onlooker shouted, "In your Catholicism all treason is contained." Tolerance is a hard lesson to learn and about 250 people died for their faith during Elizabeth's reign. The majority of Catholics were of course not hounded to death, but the "blind eye" habits of the early part of the reign gave way to harsh penalties—such as £20 fines for not attending Church, or 100 Marks for going to Mass, or seizure of two-thirds of their lands. England did not become Catholic again despite the efforts of the Jesuits, but the remaining Catholics had their faith bolstered and many of their descendants have stayed faithful to this day.

If Elizabeth's Church of England was not accepted by Catholics, it was also rejected by the Puritans. There were those like Thomas Cartwright who wanted to get rid of bishops and have elected elders and appointed ministers ruling the church at various levels from a local church up to a national assembly; these were called Presbyterians. Others wanted each local church to be its own master; their leader was Robert Browne and they were called Brownists, although today we would call them Congregationalists. The Puritans as a whole ranted against anything connected with Roman Catholicism. A surplice was branded as the "livery of Anti-Christ". They fumed against organs and choirs—"The service of God is grievously abused by piping with organs, singing, ringing . . . and the squeaking of chanting choristers." Even the use of a ring in marriage and the cross at a baptism were frowned upon.

The Arts

Religious changes—the swing of the pendulum

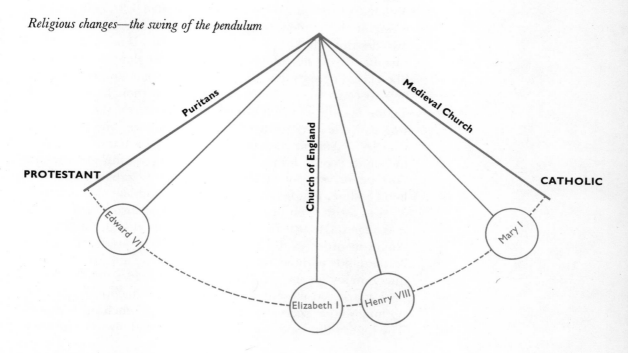

Elizabeth had no use for such ideas. Catholic she might not be, but she liked her crosses and candles and disliked these serious-minded men who persisted in lecturing her. They had too little respect for royalty for her liking. People like Cartwright were sent into exile, a small number, some five of them, were executed, and Archbishop Whitgift set about purging the Church of England of its Puritan clergy. For the time being they were brought to heel or left the Church, but the Puritan laymen could not be so easily dealt with. Once again religion and politics were mixed up and many Puritan gentry learned to oppose Elizabeth in Parliament. She used all her feminine wiles, her native wit and her royal temper to keep them in their place, but as her reign closed they were still baying at her from the floor of the House of Commons. Whoever succeeded her would have to face similar opposition.

The Tale of Three Queens and Foreign Princes

Religion and politics were just as mixed in foreign affairs as they were at home. Elizabeth could not afford to tempt fate by trumpeting her Protestantism abroad for fear the Pope would call for a crusade against England. She kept the Pope quiet for thirteen years and used every trick to persuade Catholic France, Austria and Spain that, given time, England might yet return to the Catholic fold. Marriages were part of diplomacy and unlike most royal women, Elizabeth was no pawn in the marriage-diplomacy game. She controlled her own destiny. The title—the Virgin Queen—is not just a quirk. Elizabeth used her unmarried state to England's advantage. She played up outrageously to Philip of Spain and encouraged him to court her, enticing him with the thought of another Tudor marriage which would regain for him the throne of England. He tired of her apparent fickleness and Archduke Charles of Austria was encouraged to try his hand—receiving the same "come hither" and "some other time" treatment. Parliament was not at all happy about Elizabeth's spinster-hood and her first fierce quarrel with them blew up when they tried to insist upon her marriage. Her last throw in the royal marriage stakes was in 1580 when she flirted with the Duke of Anjou in order to divert the French from interfering in the Netherlands without risking the goodwill of France. It was a queer match for she was twenty-one years older than the ugly, pock-marked duke but, like other "loves" before, it came to nothing and it succeeded in keeping the French on her side. The Queen did have her loves, but her head always ruled her heart. She might well have lost both over Robert Dudley, Earl of Leicester, who carried on a passionate courtship with Elizabeth. The Queen only just avoided a scandal when his wife died mysteriously. Common sense prevailed and she stopped the affair. Her last love was stopped even more drastically. Robert Devereux, Earl of Essex, chose to flatter her in her old age and then chose to plot a rising because his ambitions were thwarted. She had his head instead of his heart. Tudors put loyalty above love.

The Earl of Essex

Elizabeth avoided open war for seventeen years with one exception. This was her attempt to win back Calais in 1562 and to weaken France by encouraging a religious civil war. She failed, but even her trying compared favourably with Mary's loss of Calais and it taught her too that England could not afford the luxury of a war. In any case, even if France was the traditional enemy, Spain was becoming more of a real threat and France was the obvious counter. If Elizabeth put England before her heart she also put her country before any religious beliefs. The French alliance became very necessary. France was drifting into a civil war between the Protestant Huguenots and the Catholic government and it would have been natural for Elizabeth to help her fellow Protestants. France too was ruled, in all but name, by a woman, *Catherine de Medici*, the Queen Mother, who felt in many ways like Elizabeth. She was a Catholic, yet she feared Catholic Spain as much as the Protestant Huguenots, and an alliance with Protestant England became necessary for her. Catherine and Elizabeth had just signed a treaty of alliance in 1572 when the affairs of the Night of St. Bartholomew nearly wrecked this

The St. Bartholomew Massacre

John Knox

Mary, Queen of Scots

alliance of Queens. Catherine tried to solve her Protestant problem by brutal murder and on this night the Huguenot leaders, who were in Paris for a royal wedding, were massacred in their beds. Elizabeth protested. Her Court went into mourning, but she did nothing more and the French alliance survived to be used in her game of divide and defend against the Catholic powers. The idea that women let their emotions run away with them is given the lie by Catherine and Elizabeth. One fancies that kings would have gone to war in a surge of religious fervour, queens wept and stayed at home.

Elizabeth could count herself lucky that domestic strife and a shrewd ruler, the French Queen Mother, would prevent French interference in English affairs. Another possible source of trouble was Scotland and here too we see unsettled times and a queen on the throne, but this one was to prove far more of a handful for Elizabeth than the French ruler. Civil war flared up in Scotland in 1560 when the Calvinists, led by John Knox, turned against the Scottish government and Elizabeth was only too pleased to help them seize power. She feared that the traditional friendship between Scotland and France might be used against England in the future as it had been in the past. There were good grounds for her fears for *Mary Stuart*, the young Scottish Queen, had married Francis II of France. She was a fervent Catholic and she had a very good claim to the English throne as well. Her grandmother had been a daughter of Henry VII. A Scottish government which was anti-Catholic and anti-French would suit Elizabeth's purpose and keep in check any ambitions Mary, Queen of Scots, might have.

Mary did have ambitions. In fact in 1560 she seemed to have most things—youth, beauty, power and faith—but within three years she had nothing but memories and a bleak future. Her beauty, her long imprisonment and her sad end began the myth that she was a poor injured soul wronged by everybody, but Mary brought many of her tragedies upon herself. She had an unhappy knack of doing the wrong thing at the worst possible time, and unfortunately it was a family trait which her Stuart descendants brought with them when they became kings of England. Her husband died when she was eighteen and she had to return to Scotland in 1561. She had been in France for most of her life and the new stern Calvinist government was not at all to her liking.

She started sensibly and did nothing to give John Knox and his followers any grounds for complaint, although they tried hard to find fault with the lovely young Queen. She did nothing to rouse Elizabeth's fears and she kept any hopes she

36

might have of becoming Queen of England very quiet. Within twelve months all this was changed. She deliberately provoked Elizabeth by marrying her cousin, Henry Stuart, Lord Darnley, who also had a claim to the English throne. She had the Calvinists after her blood too when she called for a Catholic crusade to make Scotland Catholic once more. She soon reaped the reward of her rash marriage for her very real love for Darnley turned to hate because of his wild jealousy and stupid character. He was in the plot to have her secretary, David Rizzio, murdered before her eyes.

Lord Burghley

Soon after her son was born, the future James VI of Scotland and James I of England, Darnley was mysteriously murdered. The house in which he lay ill was blown up and he was discovered strangled in the garden. We do not know if Mary was directly concerned with this plot but she was very foolish to marry the leader of it, the Earl of Bothwell. She was married, too, in a Protestant Church and therefore lost the support of the Pope and the sympathy of Catholic Europe. The best one can say is that she loved the rascal Bothwell but, as Elizabeth knew only too well, queens cannot afford to let their hearts rule. The rebels were up in arms. Mary was forced to abdicate and was imprisoned in Lochleven Castle. The infant, James, was made king.

Twelve months later, in 1568, Mary had escaped from Lochleven, with the assistance of her gaoler who had fallen for her charms, and she tried to win back her crown. She failed, the Regent Murray routed her army and she fled across the border and flung herself on the mercy of Elizabeth. From now on all the romantic tales are all in favour of the "Queen of Hearts" and against Elizabeth, yet Mary's enforced visit was the last thing Elizabeth wanted. Her natural allies were the Scottish Calvinists, but she could not approve of a queen being deposed by her subjects. Someone might be tempted to do the same in England. At the same time she could not put Mary back on the throne with English troops, or she would betray her own Protestant cause. She could not even ship Mary back to France for here she would be the willing tool of plotters against Elizabeth's throne and she could not quietly "dispose" of her for fear of bringing the might of Catholic France and Spain against England. In the end Elizabeth did virtually nothing—she had a "hearing" at York when the Scottish Regent Murray was called to put his case against Mary and she was asked to deny it. It was a farce and the decision was a vague "not proven". Elizabeth stalled for time, hoping that events in Scotland might restore Mary, but this never happened and instead Mary passed her time in a wearisome "honourable captivity" in a number of castles—amongst them Carlisle, Sheffield and Tutbury. Her conditions were by no means unpleasant, but her presence in England made her the centre of plots to overthrow Elizabeth and it must be admitted that she agreed with many of them.

Elizabeth's relations with Spain gradually worsened from 1568. In 1569 a plot hatched by De Spes, the Spanish Ambassador, was discovered and in the same year the Northern Earls tried a Catholic rising in Durham, with the recognition of Mary as Elizabeth's heir as one of its aims. Elizabeth's ministers coped with the rising and it was crushed. The Ridolfi plot of 1571 to assassinate Elizabeth and put Mary on the throne implicated Mary and the leading Catholic noble, the Duke of Norfolk. In that year, the Pope excommunicated Elizabeth and the years of prolonged calm were over. Parliament wanted Elizabeth to have Mary's head there and then but she refused. Dog does not eat dog, queen does not kill queen, only Norfolk was executed. The Queens endured each other for sixteen more years, with Walsingham's secret service discovering more plots.

Mary was eventually tricked into betraying herself. An amateurish plot, formed by Anthony Babington, was rooted

The execution of Mary, Queen of Scots,
in the Great Hall at Fotheringay

out but was allowed to go on, carefully watched by Walsingham. A spy planted in Mary's Court delivered into Walsingham's hands the letter from her agreeing to the assassination of Elizabeth. Babington was sent to the block and Mary, tried for her part in the plot, was found guilty. To the last Elizabeth tried to avoid the death sentence, but Parliament stormed and Elizabeth wavered. She signed the warrant hurriedly and the messenger sped on his way to Fotheringay Castle, where, in February 1587, Mary's unhappy life was ended. Elizabeth protested that the Council had betrayed her, that the warrant should never have been sent—who knows? Mary's death was the last straw for Philip of Spain. England and Spain had been at war in the Netherlands and on the open sea since 1585, now Philip made up his mind that he would rid himself of the accursed English and their Queen once and for all.

"God blew and they were scattered"

This title is taken from the medal which Elizabeth had struck to commemorate the defeat of the Armada. It was not only in the sixteenth century that nations at war always thought that God was on their side. Certainly both Elizabeth and Philip thought their cause was right and that God must be for them, and often what people think is happening is as important as what really is happening. It would be easy to say that England and Spain went to war because Elizabeth was Protestant and Philip was Catholic, but this would be only part of the story. Elizabeth's England had been Protestant for twenty-seven years without Spain raising a religious crusade against it. It was only when religious rivalry was fanned by other quarrels that war began.

Transport by Sea
Art of War

England was jealous of the big share of the New World which Spain had taken and of the flow of silver and gold from the rich mines of South America. Twice a year a great convoy of treasure ships sailed to Spain—the "flota" sailed from San Juan de Ulua in the Gulf of Mexico bringing Mexican treasure, and the "galleones" from Nombre de Dios bringing silver from Perus. All the year mule trains crossed the Isthmus carrying their precious loads to the assembly ports. It was the French who first used pirate tactics to raid such rich spoils, but the English sea dogs from ports in the South and West were quick to follow suit. From the 1540's onward there was no peace beyond the "lines", that is the Canaries meridian and the Tropic of Cancer, and although governments in Europe might be at peace, on the high seas it was every man for himself and the devil take the hindmost.

A Spanish Flagship

Hawkins and Drake

Industry and Trade

Hawkins

John Hawkins was a Plymouth man, the son of a merchant. He was a charming man, an excellent seaman, a capable administrator and unlike most English "sea dogs" he was modest, lacking their usual conceit and rashness. He hoped to break into the trade with the Spanish Empire by peaceful means by giving the Spanish colonists the goods they wanted. The "goods" they wanted above all others were "men", and Hawkins made use of the so-called triangle of trade: the Outward Passage from England to Guinea, the Middle Passage from Guinea carrying slaves to the West Indies, and the Homeward Passage from the West Indies to England. Slavery is a dreadful thing in our eyes, but it was quite acceptable to people in the less squeamish sixteenth century. His first two voyages were a success, but their success was their undoing for Spain wanted such trade to belong to Spaniards. In 1567 his third fleet met disaster. His main ship, a decrepit veteran donated by the Queen and named the *Jesus of Lubeck*, was damaged and he put into San Juan de Ulua for repairs just as the "flota" was expected. Hawkins used this event to

The Atlantic

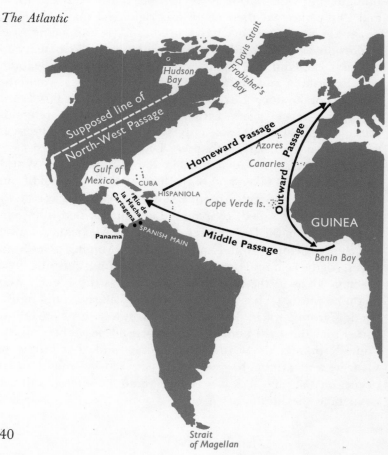

bargain with the Spaniards, promising to leave the treasure ships alone if they would not trouble him. The Spaniards broke their word, attacked Hawkins' fleet, destroying all but two ships, the *Minion* and the *Judith*, commanded by the young Francis Drake. In a sense this started the war with Spain for from now on the English "privateers" and the Spanish were at each other's throats. They were called "privateers" because they were private adventurers and not officially recognised by Elizabeth's government. But although she might assure the Spanish Ambassador that she disapproved of these "pirates", the wily Elizabeth was always ready to take her share of the spoils. Hawkins' active days were almost finished, but he returned home to a shore job. He administered and reconstructed the navy in preparation for the struggle which was bound to come. He came out of retirement to command the *Victory* against the Armada and he eventually died at sea in 1595 when he went with Drake on a West Indian raid against the "Dons".

Francis Drake was only just a Devon man. for his family moved to Chatham in Kent when he was very young. He came to stand for everything Elizabethan—an excellent sea-man, a gallant fighter who could be merciful in victory, cocksure, and brash, but with a burning faith in England, its Protestant religion and its vigorous Queen. To Englishmen he was a hero, to the Spaniards he was a cut-throat and a pirate. His first clash with the Spaniards was under Hawkins at San Juan de Ulua, and if he had doubted that they were treacherous, events there convinced him of this fact. He "privateered" in 1570 and 1571 in the Spanish Main and got enough booty to whet his appetite for more. His big moment, however, came a year later when with Elizabeth's secret blessing, he raided Nombre de Dios and then, forsaking his beloved sea for the less friendly land, he led a foraging party into the Isthmus of Panama, waylaid a treasure train and took to his ships again, £40,000 better off. Elizabeth and Philip were beginning to be more friendly by this time, and although this was only a temporary phase, it would have embarrassed Elizabeth if Drake had carried out any more exploits. He spent a few quiet years in Ireland, but by 1577 he was once more on his bridge and sailing for new seas. The plan was to sail through the Strait of **Magellan**, raid the ill-defended Pacific coast and then sail home through the so-called North-West Passage, always providing that he could discover the passage, for its existence was only hearsay. *Sebastian Cabot* had tried and failed, and *Frobisher* was probing for it in 1576 and was de-

Sir Francis Drake

41

luded into thinking he had found its eastern end. Drake's ship, the *Golden Hind*, originally the *Pelican*, was accompanied by two others but before they had sailed round South America, he had to quell a mutiny and execute one of the captains, Thomas Doughty. No sooner was he through the Strait than high winds and swelling seas robbed him of his companion ships. The *Golden Hind* continued on alone and then fortune smiled again. In the March of 1578 they sighted and sank the treasure ship *Cacafuego*. Drake landed in California and claimed it for Elizabeth in the name of "New Albion", and sailed for the North-West Passage, but discovered there was no such route home. Drake turned westward again and sailed for Asia, reaching the "Spice Islands" in 1579. Then he sailed on across the Indian Ocean, round Africa and so home by 1580. His voyage had taken three years and he was the first Englishman to sail round the world. Apart from fame, Drake brought back handsome profits for his backers. They received £47 for every £ they had invested. Elizabeth, too, waited with her hands out for her share of the spoils and flying in the face of her usual caution taunted Philip by knighting Drake on his own ship at Deptford.

Open war with Spain was only just round the corner and it was the exploits of men like Drake which hastened the fight. In 1586, with swashbuckling defiance, the newly appointed "General of Her Majesty's Navy" tore through the West Indies like a tornado. San Domingo and Carthagena were captured and sacked, and Philip was hard put to it to restore the towns. Drake's story is now part of the wider story. His greatest moments were yet to come. He was also to reach the lowest depths of despair. After the Armada, Drake fell into disgrace and in some ways died in it. The ill-fated Drake–Hawkins expedition of 1595 killed them both. He found no Valhalla death fighting against his hated foes, but died miserably of dysentery off Porto Bello on 28th January, 1596. He was buried at sea as befits a "sea dog". If you read Newbolt's poem "Drake's Drum" you can feel the dash and vigour of a magnificent sailor and a great Elizabethan.

In most countries in Northern Europe men were beginning to realise that they had many things in common with their neighbours: language, religion, culture and even enemies. This sense of belonging together is called nationalism and to be a Spaniard or an Englishman was to feel special and rather cocksure, despising men from other lands. By the middle of the sixteenth century, nationalism was well rooted in countries like France, Spain and England, but in other parts of Europe

A Spanish captain

42

the tender plant was only just pushing through. It is rare that a nation wins a place in the sun for itself without a struggle for there are always overlord nations ready to deny it a place. The provinces of the Spanish Empire which were called The Netherlands, particularly the seven northern provinces which were Dutch speaking and Protestant preaching, had grown tired of the overlordship of Spain. Throughout the 1560s, the Netherlands had been restless, pirate ships raided Spanish ships in the Channel and a steady trickle of refugees crossed over to England. The Netherlands were important to England, the rich wool trade with Flanders was one of England's mainstays. Elizabeth was only too ready to stir up trouble so long as she did not have to do it openly. On one occasion in 1568 she even confiscated a Spanish fleet loaded with pay for the Duke of Alva's troops and bound for the Netherlands. In 1572 the provinces finally revolted and were led by the capable William of Orange, perhaps better known as William the Silent.

Industry and Trade

Elizabeth might have been tempted to ally with William, but her policy was to harass Philip and not to challenge him directly. England could not afford the luxury of open war. She did her best to avoid taking sides and the Dutch struggled on alone. By 1575 Elizabeth and William were almost enemies, but when the Spanish looked as though they would defeat the Dutch, Elizabeth intervened. To be exact, she paid Duke John Casimir of the Palatinate to lead a rag-tag army to help the Netherlands. William knew that such help was worse than useless and turned in despair to France for real help. There was great heart-searching at Elizabeth's Court, for French control of the Netherlands would be even worse for England than Spanish. "The only remedy left to us is prayer," said Lord Walsingham, but Elizabeth had other ideas. Once again she used her spinsterhood and wooed the French Duke of Anjou and distracted him from his true business, the making of a French kingdom in the Netherlands. In 1583 his troops, ill-used and unpaid, sacked Antwerp; Anjou retired in disgrace. The sands of time were running out, however, for both Elizabeth and William. The Spanish Duke of Parma steadily re-conquered the provinces. William was assassinated in 1584 and the long talked of Catholic alliance against Elizabeth looked like becoming a reality. Certainly, if Philip of Spain could subdue the Dutch, it would need only a pause for breath before he turned his attention to England. Elizabeth was forced to act and an English force led by the Earl of Leicester with some 6000 foot soldiers and 1000 cavalry landed in the Netherlands in 1585. It achieved very little

William the Silent

The Art of War

43

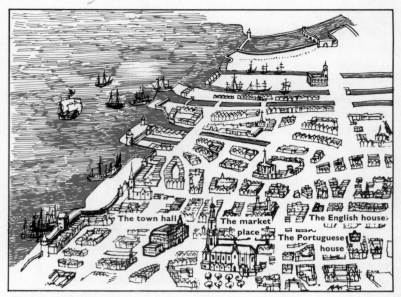

Antwerp in 1570

success, but it meant that England was now in the struggle. The years of uneasy peace gave way to years of uneasy war.

"All the world never saw a force as theirs was" is how the Commander of Elizabeth's navy, Lord Howard of Effingham, described the great fleet of galleons and transports which Philip was massing in his ports. The aim of the Armada was to sail to the Netherlands, pick up troops there and then invade England. It was common knowledge that the fleet was collecting from 1586 onwards and that its commander would probably be a renowned sailor, Santa Cruz. The English seamen were hardly the type to sit at home and wait to be shot at and Drake, with his usual cheek, carried out his most daring exploit. He sailed straight into Cadiz harbour and sank about thirty ships, and then calmly captured a fort near Cape Vincent and from this Spanish base raided Spanish supply ships. Drake was said to have singed the King of Spain's beard. Another setback was the death of Santa Cruz early in 1588. If Elizabeth had been bold enough to carry on Drake's raiding policy the Armada might not have sailed, but she became afraid for the defence of England itself and would not listen to Drake's pleas. The more cautious Lord Howard was appointed over the navy and he too was not allowed to attack. So his commanders Drake, Hawkins and Frobisher had to sit

The Art of War   it out and wait for the Armada to strike.

On 19th July, 1585, an armada, sailing in a crescent formation, was sighted off the Lizard. The news was blazed to

Plymouth and to London by beacon and carried by hard-ridden horses. The fate of England was in the balance and stayed there for nine long days before the running fight was ended. The two fleets were not as ill-matched as enthusiastic reporters liked to make out. Both sides had about the same

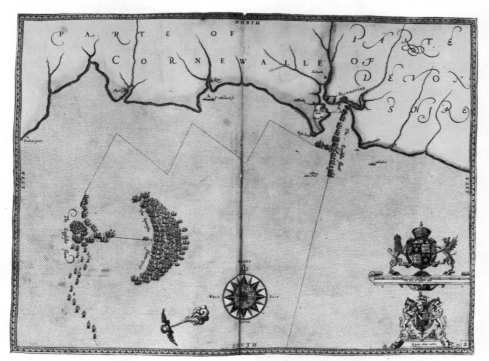

The Armada

number of ships with some fifty galleons or men-o'-war and eighty other vessels, varying from clumsy transports to tubby merchantmen. The Spanish commander was not a sailor at all. The Duke of Medina Sidonia was much happier on land and, brave though he was, he had little stomach for his particular job. The English captains, on the other hand, had salt water for blood and were itching for this moment. The crescent formation of the "Dons" was a good one and much more difficult to attack than a treasure convoy in the Caribbean. Although the lighter English ships could out-sail and out-shoot the slower Spanish ships, they could not break the Spanish line and the Armada hove-to off Calais on 17th July almost intact.

Drake's earlier exploits had shown the value of fire-ships in a confined harbour and on the following night six ships loaded with pitch and shavings were steered into the tight Spanish

Atlantic gales

Wrecks

Spanish Netherlands

Plymouth

London
Dover

Flushing
Antwerp

Gravelines

Calais

Brest

Rouen

Paris

The course of the Armada

Ferrol

Corunna

Santander

San Sebastian

Lisbon

Madrid

Sagres

Seville

The war with Spain

ranks. Panic followed, the sailors cut their moorings and sailed wildly into the blazing broadsides of Howard's fleet sailing off-shore. Medina Sidonia's flag ship was driven towards the Flemish coast and the last stand was made off Gravelines. Only four ships were sunk, but many more were crippled and thousands of men died. Even the weather was pro-English and a strong south-westerly sent the scattered Armada scudding up the east coast and to the north of Scotland. From here they doubled back into the Atlantic only to be driven by gales on to the Scottish and Irish shores. The treasure ship of Tobermory Bay is one of the many stories, some fact, some fiction, which the wrecked fleet has left in its wake. The extent of the English victory can be exaggerated. The English captains were disappointed at the lack of damage done for at least half of the Spanish ships limped back to Spain. Certainly the Spanish navy was not destroyed and was still a force to be reckoned with. Above all, however, England was safe, and a new chapter in England's history had opened. A glimpse of Elizabeth's greatness peeps through ten days after the Armada, when a false alarm raised the militia at Tilbury. Queen Bess, dressed in armour, inspected her troops and loving the drama of the moment spoke to her men: "I know I have the body of a weak and feeble woman but I have the heart and stomach of a king and of a King of England too and I think foul scorn that . . . Spain or any prince of Europe should dare to invade the borders of my realm." The Tudors were part of their times and every able-bodied Englishman would have said, "Hear, hear" to her speech.

This is the picture of Elizabeth which recalls a well-loved Queen. There is another side to the picture. The war with Spain dragged on, religious toleration was no nearer. Prices were rising and the Court could hardly make ends meet. Furthermore, the early colonies like Virginia were a failure. But when all is said and done, Elizabeth's reign is an affectionate chapter in our history. She summed it up for herself in her last speech to Parliament:

"And though God hath raised me high, yet this I account the glory of my Crown, that I have reigned with your loves."

"Gloriana" died in the early hours of 24th March, 1603, clinging to life to the end. She passed on her crown to James Stuart, King of Scotland. Her last act was her worst.

A galleon of the Armada being driven ashore by gales

The
Wisest Fool in
Christendom

James I

Government

JAMES I (1603–25)

"He was naturally of a timorous disposition, which was the reason for his quilted doublet. His beard was very thin, his tongue too large for his mouth . . . his skin was soft as taffeta, which felt so because he never washed his hands . . . his legs were very weak." James Stuart, the Sixth of Scotland and the First of England, did not look the stuff of which kings are made, and certainly the robust Tudor strain in his blood had been swamped by lesser breeds and the beauty of his Stuart mother was not reflected in his puny face. If he did not look the part nor did he act it, for although he was well intentioned, kind and thoughtful, he was a poor judge of men and a worse judge of circumstances. He was everything the Tudors were not, he was "The wisest fool in Christendom".

If he had been the wisest man in Christendom he would have found it hard to reign successfully. Elizabeth willed him £200, three thousand dresses and a debt of £400,000 with a grumbling Parliament who would help out financially only at the price of a greater share in government. In Elizabeth's time Parliament was a restless servant of the Crown, now it wanted to be an equal partner. Many Members of Parliament were Puritans who would not accept the still new Church of England. Money, politics and religion were capable of rousing great passions and together they were, and still are, dynamite.

James's character and his Scottish upbringing did not help him to deal with such an explosive situation. He had brought his Scottish subjects to heel and relished doing the same to his new subjects. He came to the throne with a marked sense of his own importance. James did not invent the "Divine Right of Kings", for in all ages kings have seen themselves either as gods or particularly blessed by God. He was learned enough, however, to write up a common practice into a theory and in

48

a well-reasoned pamphlet called, "The mystical reverence that belongs unto Him that sit on the Throne of God", he spelled out what it meant—"The King is King in himself and by no assent of his subjects".

He was foolish enough to fling such ideas at Parliament and failed to recognise that England would not accept in his day what it had accepted as normal even fifty years before.

James thought that the Church of England, with the King as its Head, would be a much better prop for his ambitions than the Presbyterian Church of Scotland and he was determined to give it his support. On the other hand, the Catholics hoped that the son of Mary Queen of Scots would be well disposed to them, and the Puritans expected a welcome from a Presbyterian King. James was tolerant and willing not to enforce the laws against Catholic and Puritan, but was not willing to do more. The Puritans tested him on his way to London when they presented him with the Millenary Petition, asking him to reform the Church of England, and James called them to a conference at Hampton Court. He made his views quite plain in his famous "No bishop, no king" speech, that if bishops were destroyed the King would receive the same treatment. Puritan hopes were destroyed instead. He ordered them to conform or he would "harry them out of the land" and a number of them took him at his word and fled to Leyden in Holland, and later set sail in the *Mayflower* to the New World. The one useful thing which came from the Hampton Court conference was the Authorised Version of the Bible, which James had scholars prepare and which was published in 1611. You will probably find a copy on your bookshelves today.

The Catholics were even more disappointed. The tolerance of the first year of his reign gave way to still harsher enforcement of the laws against them. Priest hunting became fashionable again. In their anger they plotted his and Parliament's downfall. The Gunpowder Plot of 1605 is one event which everyone remembers, but the annual burning of Guy Fawkes is only half of the story.

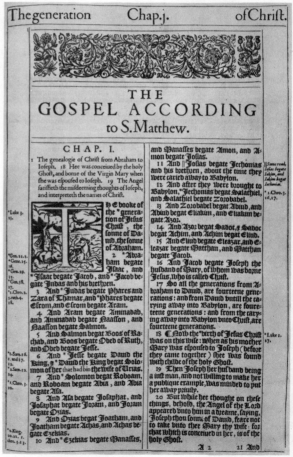

The Mayflower

A page from the Authorised Version of the Bible, 1611

The Guy Fawkes conspirators

Bates
Robert Winter
Christopher Wright
John Wright
Thomas Percy
Guido Fawkes
Robert Catesby
Thomas Winter

Guy Fawkes was only the soldier of fortune who was to put the finishing touches to the plot by lighting the thirty-six barrels of gunpowder. A group of Roman Catholic gentry led by Robert Catesby planned to destroy the King and Parliament and then to seize power and put James's daughter, Elizabeth, on the throne. One of the plotters feared for the life of a relative, Lord Monteagle, who was a Member of Parliament and sent him a warning note. Monteagle hurried to the Earl of Salisbury with it a week before the plot was timed to start. It seems that Guy Fawkes had been warned of the danger, but still hoped to pull it off. Instead, on the evening of 4th November he was caught in the vaults of the House of Lords. Fawkes was tortured dreadfully before he was executed. Catesby and his friends had fled to Holbeach House hoping to rouse the countryside in a last desperate gamble. Some were killed whilst being captured, others were treated like Guy Fawkes and died painfully. The

The letter of betrayal

plot and its failure killed any hopes of Roman Catholics being tolerated for some time.

James did not want this anti-Catholic feeling to interfere with his desire for peace abroad. One of his first acts had been to end the long war with Spain. It meant that one of Elizabeth's popular courtiers, *Sir Walter Raleigh*, was sacrificed. Sir Walter has been called the "last of the Elizabethans". He was courageous and courtly, a soldier who had fought in France, a sailor who had attacked the Spanish at Cadiz in 1596, a man of letters and a poet. He dreamed of England's expansion into the New World and tried to realise his dreams by founding a colony in Virginia in 1585, although the first attempts were fruitless. He dreamed, too, of the wealth of the New World, and believed in the existence of "El Dorado", the city of gold, which was thought to be somewhere in Guiana and ready for the taking. Unfortunately, he also believed that war with Spain was necessary, when the opposite was true, for England's expansion now needed peace; ploughs instead of swords; merchant ships not "men-o'-war". He was convicted of treason for plotting against James, but he was spared the block in 1603 and spent the next twelve years in the Tower. James's eldest son, Henry, felt the waste of such a talented man when he said, "Who but my father could keep such a bird in a cage?" James had not finished with Raleigh, however, and in 1616 he was released to try and find this "El Dorado". James could use its wealth, but there was to be no fighting the Spanish. Raleigh's city stayed a pipe dream. He sailed up the Orinoco, but came to blows with Spanish settlers and had to return empty-handed. James blew the cobwebs off the fifteen-year-old treason charge and Sir Walter was executed in 1618. He died serenely, and in his dying he showed up the mean smallness of his Stuart king.

Sir Walter Raleigh

Expansion of England

Trade and colonies flourished in the peaceful years before the Civil War. Virginia, which had failed in Elizabeth's reign, was refounded by the Virginia Company in 1607 and its capital became Jamestown. Its tobacco flourished and plantations were established which made money for English merchants and Virginian planters and misery for the imported negroes who worked the soil.

Farther north the Pilgrim Fathers landed on the shores of Cape Cod on 11th November, 1620. The idea behind this voyage of the *Mayflower* came from a group of Puritans who wanted to enjoy the independence and religious freedom denied them in England. They were a minority, however, in

Industry and Trade

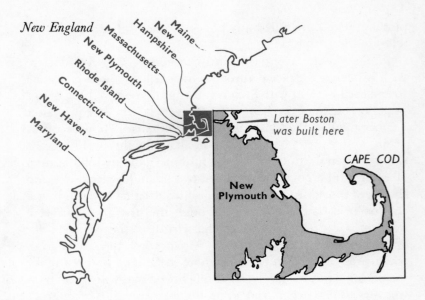

New England

Maine
New Hampshire
Massachusetts
New Plymouth
Rhode Island
Connecticut
New Haven
Maryland

Later Boston
was built here

CAPE COD

New
Plymouth

the ship and in the colony, for the "Saints" numbered only seventeen men, nine women and fourteen children, whilst the rest, Merchant Venturers and Church of England to boot, numbered seventeen men, ten women and fourteen children and were accompanied by five hired men and twelve indentured servants. This first settlement was called New Plymouth and it was followed by New Hampshire and Maine (1622), Massachusetts (1629), Maryland (1632), Rhode Island (1636), New Haven (1638) and Connecticut (1639). These were seafaring and farming colonies and quite different from Virginia.

This was a time, too, when English traders were pushing into far corners of the globe. By 1650, English trading posts, or factories, were scattered from Persia to India, and from Madagascar to the East Indies. The East India Company was typical of the way the traders joined together and financed their voyages. It was given a charter in 1600 and its members started by taking part in single voyages and then drawing profit from that voyage. Soon money was raised to cover a number of voyages over a number of years and eventually it became a joint stock company, in which members invested their money permanently and drew their profits. The East Indiamen hoped to trade mainly for spices with the East Indies, but the Dutch had other ideas and all was fair in love, war and trade. The end of this hope came at Amboyna, an English trading post referred to as a "factory", in 1623. Eighteen English traders at this "factory" were horribly tortured and ten of them executed. After this the English concentrated on India, where their Portuguese rivals were easier to

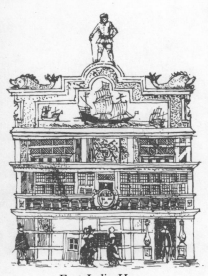

East India House

52

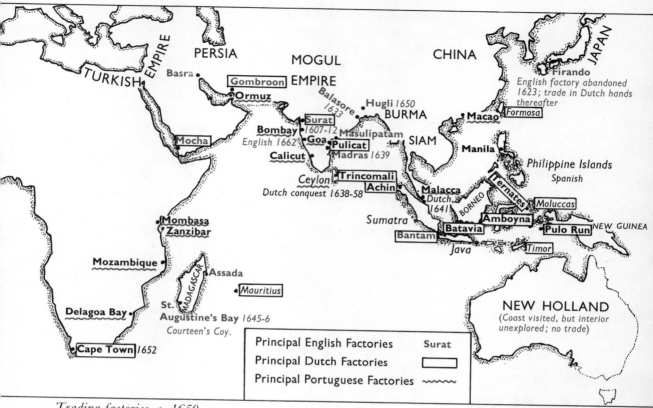

Trading factories, c. 1650

deal with than the Dutch. Factories at Surat and Madras were the forerunners of many more and were the start of the British Empire in India, but that story belongs to the next century.

In another way, too, Raleigh had the last laugh, for James's plans for the marriage of his son Charles to the Infanta Maria of Spain came to nothing. Prince Henry had died in 1612 and James tried to win allies by arranging the right sort of marriages for his children. In 1613 he married his daughter Elizabeth to Frederick, the Elector of the Palatinate, and the leading Protestant prince in Germany. By 1618 Europe was plunged into a war which was to last thirty years, and Frederick was in the middle of it. He accepted an invitation to become the luckless King of Bohemia in 1619, and the Austrian Emperor, the overlord of Bohemia, promptly deposed him and chased him from his own land.

In 1621 James called Parliament for the third time in his reign and he hoped they would give him a large grant to help Frederick. They did nothing of the sort, instead they ranted against the illegal way he had raised money. The usual way to raise money was for Parliament to grant the King "tunnage and poundage", or customs duty. James found this was not enough and imposed further duties; he sold monopolies, or sole rights, to men who sold or made anything from nails to soap. They turned their anger on Lord Chancellor Bacon, famous as a philosopher and scientist as well as a statesman, and impeached him. Impeachment had not been used since the middle of the fifteenth century and was an accusation made by Parliament and tried by Parliament. They found Bacon guilty of corruption, fined him and sentenced him to prison, and although James managed to reprieve him from these charges, he was driven from office. Parliament had shown the King that they intended to control his officers. They went on to try to control the King's policy too, asking him to marry his son to a Protestant, declare war on Spain and renew the old naval war, though how that would help a German prince is hard to see. James was furious and brought out the high flown words of Divine Right only to have them flung back at him—"the liberties, franchise, privileges and jurisdiction of Parliament are the ancient and undoubted birthright of the subjects of England." James tore this protest from the pages of the Commons Journal, but he could not tear it from men's minds.

James had enough common sense to know when to climb down, and the failure of his son Charles's trip to Spain to woo the Infanta personally made him tread warily. Charles and Buckingham, a thoroughly disliked royal favourite, had set out for Madrid with high hopes—"Two dear adventurous knights worthy to be put in a new romance" so James described them. They got a cool reception and some red-hot demands for the freedom of worship for English Catholics, and on their return to England they both urged the King to drop the proposed marriage and agree to Parliament's suggestion. War was declared in 1624 and Parliament gave James £300,000 to fight it with. The grant was nowhere near enough; it enabled a poor army to reach Dover en route to Europe, but there the money gave out, and the expedition got no farther than Flushing.

James died in 1625. The fate of the nation was in the balance. During the twenty-two years of his reign, Englishmen were beginning to take sides, both King and Parliament were talking loudly of their rights, and not much was heard of their responsibilities. It would need a cool hand at the helm to steer the ship of state through these troubled waters.

An engraving of a London tobacconist's shop, 1617

"A Mild and Gracious Prince" or "A Man of Blood"?

CHARLES I (1625—49)

Was Charles I a murderer or a martyr? The anger and passions of a civil war meant that neither Roundhead nor Cavalier could give a true answer. The vantage point of three centuries seems to show that he was neither. He was honest and cultured, brave and kind, but he was also proud and stubborn, weak and rash. He was faced by an unruly Parliament and changes in thinking which made his ideas out-of-date and his actions dangerous. He paid dearly for his mistakes, for he was the only English king ever to be beheaded.

Charles I

Charles inherited a load of trouble along with his throne. At a time when the country was growing wealthier, the Crown was getting poorer. The need for a strong monarch had grown less as men's memories of the Wars of the Roses had faded and Spain's threat had weakened. The merchants and squires were voicing their feeling for power in noisy, outspoken Parliaments.

We have seen how niggardly they had been in meeting the cost of the Spanish War and they now turned round on the new king and blamed him and the Duke of Buckingham for the failure of the war. They objected to Charles's marriage to the fifteen-year-old Henrietta Maria, a French princess, and a Roman Catholic. They refused to grant Charles the tunnage and poundage for life, which English kings had been granted since Edward IV. A wiser man than Charles would have withdrawn from the war, for a king who has to go cap in hand to Parliament is in no position to bargain. Disaster followed disaster. Buckingham had grandiose ideas of repeating a Tudor-like victory at Cadiz, but it failed miserably. Charles's second parliament demanded the dismissal of Buckingham, and Charles was to remember his father's warning when he himself had supported the House of Commons' impeachment of Middlesex, "You are making a rod with which you will be

55

Duke of Buckingham

Government

scourged yourself." Two parliaments in two years and both sent packing was a bad start. His coffers were still empty and he had no victory abroad to increase his popularity.

Worse was to follow, for Charles, inspired by Buckingham, declared war on France on behalf of the French Protestants, the Huguenots. England fared no better than against Spain, and an expedition sent to La Rochelle was a disaster. Charles could not afford one war, and to fight two wars at once was stupid. He had to raise money by hook or by crook. Tunnage and poundage was levied despite Parliament's refusal to grant it. Troops were billeted upon people without their consent. A forced loan of £350,000 was demanded by Charles and eighty people were put into prison without a trial for refusing to pay such extractions. He still could not make ends meet, and a third parliament had to be called in 1628.

It should have been obvious that a new parliament was no more likely to give him money than the previous ones, and that it was much more likely to cause a rumpus for it now had plenty of evidence of wrong actions by the king. The misdeeds of Charles were listed in a document called "The Petition of Right". It was laid down that no freeman could be compelled to make a gift, loan or tax without the consent of Parliament, nor could he be imprisoned against the law. This Petition became one of the props of our liberties, but it settled nothing at the time. It said what the king could not do, but it had nothing to say on the question—who should rule, King or Parliament?

Charles reluctantly signed the Petition, as his need for money was desperate. Then Parliament granted him a subsidy, an emergency grant, but continued to fan the flames by restricting tunnage and poundage to a yearly grant and by repeating their demand for the impeachment of Buckingham. Lastly, it introduced a new, and a dangerous, religious note by criticising the ritual and religious practices of the Court, which Puritan M.P.s, like Sir John Eliot, said were "Popish".

The fate of the Duke of Buckingham was settled out of Parliament. He was stabbed in 1628 at Portsmouth by John Felton, a naval lieutenant and a Puritan, who was roused to the point of madness by the failure of the expedition to La Rochelle. The other grievances were paraded again in 1629. Eliot had called Buckingham "The grievance of grievances" but now that he had gone, there were other "grievances" on which Parliament could concentrate.

Charles was tired of parliaments—"They are of the nature of cats, they ever grow cursed with age," he said, and adjourned

Parliament. The scene which followed showed how far apart King and Parliament were. Eliot led the Commons in refusing the adjournment. The King's servants were locked out whilst inside the Speaker was not allowed to close the session until these resolutions had been passed. The resolutions laid it down that anyone who introduced religious changes towards "Popery", or advised the King to levy tunnage and poundage without Parliament's consent, should be guilty of treason. Thirdly, anyone who paid illegal levies was "a betrayer of the liberties of England".

"Popery", "Liberty", "Tyranny", these are the sort of slogans which appeal to men's emotions not their reason, and it is emotion which prompts men to fight civil wars. The next eleven years were to see these emotions build up. Before 1629, Parliament provided a safety valve, where noise and protest let off the steam of anger, but from 1629 to 1640 there was no Parliament.

"The Eleven Years' Tyranny" (1629–40)

In the sense that Charles levied taxes without Parliament's consent and made laws by his own command, the years 1629–40 were a tyranny, but it would be wrong to think that Charles became a sort of royal ogre, mumbling "off with his head" over dinner like the fairy-tale Queen of Hearts. He tried to rule fairly and efficiently. His rule is summed up best of all in the lives of his two chief advisers, Thomas Wentworth, better known as Lord Strafford, and William Laud, later Archbishop of Canterbury.

Thomas Wentworth was the son of a wealthy Yorkshire land-owner. He was educated at St John's College, Cambridge, and trained for the law at the Inner Temple. He became an M.P. for Yorkshire in 1614 and became one of the leaders in the House of Commons until he moved to the House of Lords in 1629. Wentworth had supported Parliament when it drew up the Petition of Right and had been imprisoned for refusing to pay the forced loan. He was not anti-royalist, but he wished to see an end to the bickering between King and Parliament and, as his friend said of him, "His experience taught him that it was far safer that the King should increase in power, than that the people should gain advantage on the King." He wanted good and efficient government and thought Parliament had gone too far. His friends in the Commons shouted treachery at him, however, when he accepted a peerage from the King and from 1628 he was hated by Parliament.

Lord Strafford

57

During most of the "Eleven-Year Tyranny" Strafford was in Ireland (1633–40) as Lord Lieutenant but from 1628 to 1633 he was President of the Council of the North and virtually ruled Northern England on behalf of the King. He set out to be just, firm and efficient. He tamed overbearing land-owners in the interests of the poor and he made enemies of the powerful. He could be ruthless if he felt he was right and here he hammered out his policy of "thorough".

Government

In Ireland he did much the same thing. He tamed a turbulent country, rooted out corruption, introduced efficient but fair taxes and made those who could afford to pay for them pay up. Again he made enemies of the powerful, and "Black Tom Tyrant" was the nickname which stuck in Ireland and created a reputation for him in England.

Charles's personal rule in England was similarly "thorough", and for the first time in years there was money in the royal coffers. The Poor Law was made to work, highways were maintained, and wages and prices were controlled fairly. There was, of course, a price to be paid. Good government needs money and people rarely like paying it, even if they have a say in government. They resent it bitterly when they have no say. The way of raising money which caused most bitterness was ship money. The King had always been allowed to ask for ships, or money instead of them, from coastal towns in time of national danger. Charles wanted to strengthen the navy and gain control of the English Channel from the Dutch and from pirates. He levied ship money in 1633 from the coastal towns but extended it to all the country, inland areas as well, in 1635. Charles did strengthen the navy and the money was put to its proper use. Nevertheless its collection and the reason for it smelt of sharp practice. John Hampden, a Buckingham-shire landowner, refused to pay the twenty shillings levy as a test case, but the judges found in favour of the King and against Hampden, who was imprisoned.

Transport by Land

What Strafford's policy did for the Government, Arch-bishop Laud's policy did for the Church. *William Laud* had been President of St John's College, Oxford, and James I summed him up nicely: "He hath a restless spirit which cannot see when things are well but loves to toss and change." People dislike to be hounded and this is exactly what Laud did. He wanted to make the Church of England good and worthy of respect. He wanted its services to be filled with "some beauty of holiness" and he hated the Puritan scorn of ceremony—"'Tis superstition nowadays for any man to come with no more reverence into a church than a tinker and his

William Laud

58

bitch come into an ale-house."

He encouraged the joyful use of Sunday once church had been attended. "Anti-Christ" shouted the Puritans and pulled down the maypoles. He urged men to be moral. Drunkards and adulterers were tried by the Church Courts, even the richest in the land were fearlessly called to account for their "sins". This time the Puritans could say nothing for here, at least, they were in agreement, but the people whose misdeeds were made public hated him. He demanded absolute agreement and clergymen and laymen, professors and printers, judges and drunkards, rich men, poor men . . . all who would not conform were hounded out of their jobs and into the pillory, even out of the country and into the New World.

If Charles wanted his own rule to carry on, he had to avoid rousing too much angry opposition in the land. Shortage of money was the one thing which would make him recall Parliament and only a war was likely to cost so much. Charles and Laud followed a religious policy which brought about all these things.

John Hampden

They foolishly tried to impose their English ways upon Scotland; if 300 years of failure did not warn them, then the memory of his grandmother Mary should have restrained Charles. In 1637 the new prayer book was introduced into Scotland and the old one drawn up by John Knox was withdrawn. When the Dean tried to read it in St Giles's, Edinburgh, a maidservant, Jenny Geddes, picked up her stool and hurled it at his head. Southern Scotland was roused and the National Covenant drawn up, which rallied the Scots to defend their "kirk" against English ways. Obstinate Charles would not give an inch, even though the Covenanters were not against him, only his religious policy. He found himself with a full-blown war on his hands, The Bishops' War. He called Strafford from Ireland to raise an army, and he recalled Parliament to vote him funds.

The Long and Short of it

The first Parliament of 1640 was recorded as the Short Parliament for it lasted only three weeks. It was hardly surprising that it refused any money until ship money, illegal levies and the like had been dealt with. Charles sent it packing, but he could not do the same with the Scots. They marched over the Border, camped in Durham and demanded not only a change of policy but payment for their army. Charles could not pay his own army let alone that of his enemy and again

John Pym

he had to call Parliament, this time to last, with many changes, until 1660. It executed one king, ruled without one and restored another.

The M.P.s who assembled at Westminster in 1640 were in no mood for niceties. The King had to be disciplined and the rights of Parliament established once and for all. They did not dream of doing away with the King, however. King and Parliament would still be the recipe for government, but the balance would be in favour of "them" and not "him".

Laud and Strafford were the sacrifices demanded. John Pym, the leader of Parliament, had never forgiven Strafford for his "treachery" in joining the King; he determined on the execution of Strafford and carried it through with cold ruthlessness. Charles had given Strafford his word—"Upon the word of a King, you shall not suffer in life, honour or fortune." Pym easily persuaded the Commons to pass a Bill of Attainder for treason, but before Strafford could be executed Charles must sign it. The mob howled outside the royal palace, Strafford wrote to the King and released him from his promise and Charles, beaten and bemused, signed the fatal document— "My Lord of Strafford's condition is happier than mine." Two

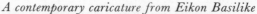

A contemporary caricature from Eikon Basilike

60

days later the King wrote a pitiful last plea. "If he must die, it were charity to reprieve him till Saturday." He was not reprieved even for so short a stay, and on Wednesday, 12th May, 1641, London sang—"His head is off"—bonfires flared. Charles lost a dear friend and gained nothing—"They promised us all should be well if my Lord Strafford's head were off and since then there is nothing better."

Archbishop Laud had been thrown into the Tower, and blessed Strafford on his way to the block. Laud's turn was to come but he stayed in prison for three years before he was executed.

Parliament now set about stripping the King of his powers— no taxes without consent, ship money declared illegal, the boundaries of the royal forests fixed, and Parliament was to be called at least once every three years; it could not be dissolved without its own consent. In 1641 it looked as if the King had been put firmly in his place.

Events then began to swing in favour of the King. Parliament was split by religious quarrels. The Puritans tried to root out bishops from the Church in their "Root and Branch" Bill, but supporters of the Church of England threw it out and the King's bold defence of the Church won him new friends from old enemies. Two parties were beginning to form—those for the King, soon known as Cavaliers, and originally a term of abuse referring to their swaggering manners, and those for Parliament, or Roundheads, a dig at the close-cropped hair of Puritan apprentices.

The title page of William Slatyer's History of Great Britain

The Puritan M.P.s determined to press on and Pym put the Grand Remonstrance before Parliament. This once again listed Charles's wrongdoings. It demanded that royal ministers should be approved by Parliament and that the Church of England should become Puritan. The Remonstrance split the Commons for it was passed, 159 for—148 against, and it swung most of the Lords to Charles.

The weeks of December were fatal in our history. A wise king would have read the signs and built up his support. Charles, urged on by his wife, Henrietta, acted rashly and triggered off the war. It was rumoured that five M.P.s were plotting to impeach the Queen. Charles rushed to her defence and ordered that the five members—Pym, Hampden, Hazelrig, Hollis and Strode, should be impeached. The House of Lords hesitated and Charles led his troops into the House of Commons itself to arrest them. Force had been paraded and the privileges of the House flaunted. It was an outrage and it was not even successful. The five M.P.s escaped across the Thames

Charles I raises the royal standard at Nottingham

and Charles commented, "I see all the birds have flown."

On 10th January, 1642, Charles left London and moved to York. Peace or war hung in the balance for six more months. In July Parliament accused Charles of raising forces against them and in August the royal standard was raised at Nottingham. War had come, and no one wanted it; a Puritan soldier expressed this hopeless mood when he wrote on the eve of battle—"God knows with what a sad sense I go upon this service and with what a perfect hatred I detest this war without an enemy."

Steps to War

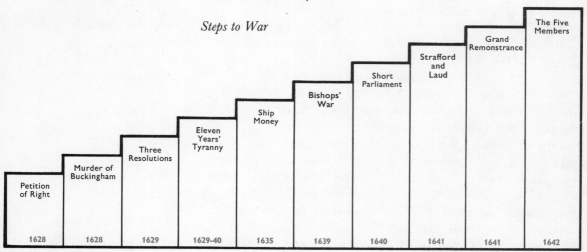

Petition of Right	Murder of Buckingham	Three Resolutions	Eleven Years' Tyranny	Ship Money	Bishops' War	Short Parliament	Strafford and Laud	Grand Remonstrance	The Five Members
1628	1628	1629	1629-40	1635	1639	1640	1641	1641	1642

The Civil War

The Civil War was really two episodes—the first "war" which lasted from 1642 to 1646, and the second which flared up in 1647 and continued for just a few months. Some parts of the country were not touched by the fighting and many people had no stake in the great rebellion. It is hard to say even which groups of people and which parts of the country fought for King or Parliament. Everywhere there were tales of families divided, of neighbouring squires supporting different sides, and of next-door neighbours at daggers drawn. A very rough division would be:

King	*Parliament*
North and West England	South, Midlands and
Wales	East
University towns	Sea ports
Country gentry	Town merchants
Anglicans	Puritans
"Commons"	"Commons"

Charles's chances of success were good, providing the war was short. Oliver Cromwell described Parliament's soldiers in 1642 as "old decayed serving men and tapsters" and the Royalist troops as "gentlemen's sons, younger sons and persons of quality." The country gentry were used to weapons and sat easy in their saddles. The early Roundhead troops, apart from the London Trained Bands, were ill-disciplined. The Cavalier leaders, too, were experienced in continental wars. Prince Rupert was a brilliant cavalry leader, and Charles himself showed early promise of making a soldier King. The Royalist High Command was united and confident in 1643. The Roundhead leaders, on the other hand, were weak. A Committee conducted the war which meant that there was no one director.

The longer the war lasted, however, the better the Roundheads' chances of success. They controlled the navy and they had more resources to pay and train their troops. The early lack of military arts was more than made up for by strong religious feelings. "Such men had the fear of God before them and made some consequence of what they did." The New Model Army grew from Cromwell's Ironsides and at last Parliament had an "army whose order and discipline, whose sobriety and manners, whose courage and success, hath made it famous and terrible all over the world."

Surprisingly enough, however, Oliver Cromwell did not

Prince Rupert

63

The Civil War, England, 1642–46

A Roundhead soldier

play a major part in the first Civil War. He was a member of the Committee. He was a captain at the Battle of Edgehill in 1642. In May 1643 he was a colonel and a lieutenant-general in the New Model Army, but even then he was second-in-command to Lord Fairfax.

In order to win, Charles had to capture London. It was not enough merely to win battles. Sixteen main battles were fought, seven were Royalist victories, eight Roundhead and one drawn, but the Cavalier successes came early without capturing the capital and the Parliamentarians' came later and wore Charles into submission.

Charles's strategy, therefore, was to advance from north and west upon London. The Earl of Essex marched out of London and pursued the royal army, but stupidly allowed it to get between himself and his base. The two forces met in the first major battle of the war at *Edgehill* in Warwickshire. Military historians will argue until doomsday whether this was a Royalist victory or a draw. Both sides were reluctant to fight, a cannon ball aimed at Charles signalled the opening of the battle at about one o'clock on 23rd October, 1642. The infantry faced each other in the centre, with light artillery, between positions, and they were flanked by the troopers. Prince Rupert was on the right flank with two regiments of horse and facing him were Ramsey's half-trained cavalry, who at the sight of the Royalist charge, turned tail and fled. Rupert chased them off the field, even pausing to plunder Kineton and this incident prevented an outright victory, for had his troops returned to the field, they would have clinched the day. The infantry in the centre reached a stalemate, in the words of the future James II, then a boy of nine and an eye-witness: "Each . . . retired some few paces and stuck down their colours, continuing to fire at one another even until night." All was confusion on the other flank—Wilmot led the Royalist charge and, like Rupert, put some of the Roundheads to flight and left the battlefield in pursuit. Meanwhile, two Roundhead cavalry regiments were unscathed and under Balfour attacked the remaining Royalist cavalry and infantry and forced them

A Royalist soldier

Plan of the Battle of Edgehill, 1642

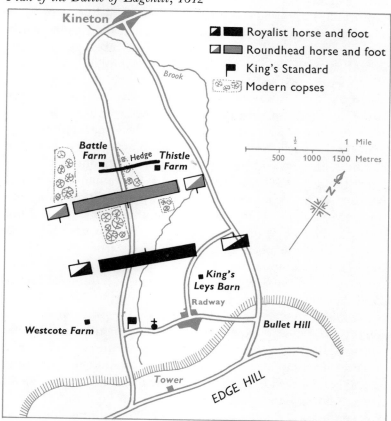

Roundhead Cavalryman

to retreat. In the mêlée, the Royal standard was captured but one Captain John Smith, of Wilmot's regiment, returning to the field spotted it and recaptured it, earning for himself a knighthood. By evening both sides were exhausted.

Essex withdrew towards Warwick and foolishly left the way to London wide open. Charles marched on and took Oxford, which he made his H.Q. for the rest of the war. This is when one of the "ifs" of history took place. If Charles had advanced on the capital as fast as he could, the course of the war and our history might have been different. He did not, however, move towards London until 13th November, by which time the Earl of Essex was back in the city and Parliament's forces out-numbered the King's. Charles withdrew from Turnham Green and the chance of victory had slipped from his fingers.

We must be content with a survey of the next three years for we would need a book to tell the full story of the Great Rebellion. In 1643 Charles launched his three-pronged attack on London from the south-west, the west and the north, but it came to nothing. A series of running battles in Yorkshire and East Anglia was indecisive, and the Royalists could not capture Hull. A similar pattern can be seen in the south-west where Plymouth held out against the Cavaliers, and in the west where Gloucester stood firm. Prince Rupert did capture Bristol, however, and this part of the campaign came to a climax at the first battle of *Newbury* (1643). Like Edgehill, this battle did not give a clear-cut victory. The King's army ran out of ammunition, and Parliament's forces under Essex were able to retire towards London again. The year 1643 closed with the Royalists apparently in a winning position, but time was marching on and they were no nearer London.

In January 1644 the Scots joined Parliament's side and besieged York. Prince Rupert hurried to its relief and entered the city easily. His troops were outnumbered but this did not stop the dashing young commander from tempting fate and moving into the open to do battle at *Marston Moor*. Lord Fairfax commanded the Roundheads and had with him Cromwell and the "Ironsides", who were of a different mettle from the raw recruits who had faced Rupert at Edgehill. The Scots were ably led by Leslie. The battle was the hardest fought of the war, some 4000 men were killed and 1500 captured. It was also one of the most confused and at one stage all six commanders had either fled from the field of battle or had been forced to retire to tend their wounds. One of them, Leven, did not stop until he reached Leeds, and Lord Fairfax was said to have fled home and to bed! The fighting continued under a harvest moon and it was Lord Fairfax's son, Thomas, and Oliver Cromwell who swung the fight for the Roundheads.

In one fell swoop the North of England was lost to Charles. Parliament's morale soared and they wanted to get rid of their aged and useless commanders. They did it by the Self-Denying Ordinance. By it, all members of Parliament agreed to lay down their commands. A new army, the New Model Army, was to be formed and Sir Thomas Fairfax was appointed General with Cromwell as his second-in-command. Its colours were scarlet, the official colours of the army to this day. It was well-armed, well-trained and well-paid, but it still had its faults, for it was composed of the veteran troops of the Earls of Essex and Manchester and its new recruits were often pressed men. The men of Kent mutinied at being forced to join up in this way. Nevertheless the quality of its leaders and the religious devotion of its hard core gave Parliament an army second to none.

The end came for the Royalists in 1645. Fairfax harried Charles in the Midlands and the two armies finally faced each other at *Naseby*. In some ways the pattern was similar to Edgehill and Marston Moor, with the New Model Army as the big difference. Prince Rupert attacked their left flank and after stiff hand-to-hand sword fighting, succeeded in driving back Ireton's troopers. In the centre the Royalist

Plan of the Battle of Naseby, 1645

infantry had early successes and, but for the resolute tactics of "Fiery Tom" Fairfax, might have carried the day. As it was their advance was halted. On the right the formidable Cromwell swept into the inferior numbered Royalists and swung the attack to the centre. If Charles had flung in his reserves the day might have been saved, but he did not. Naseby was a victory for Parliament, in fact *the* victory, for after it the Royalist cause was lost.

Government

The war ticked on for twelve more months. Hope flared for a time in Scotland, where the Royalists under the Earl of Montrose gained the upper hand over the "Covenanters", but he too was defeated in the autumn of 1645. On 5th May, 1646, after travelling in disguise with two retainers from Oxford, Charles I surrendered to the Scots at Newark.

The Second Civil War (1648)

During the first Civil War four contestants had emerged, not two—King and Parliament started it, but by 1646 the New Model Army and the Scots were powers in their own rights. Charles was defeated but not humbled. In his heart he believed that his time would come and he echoed the words of Colonel Morgan towards the end of the war, when he said to his Roundhead captors: "You have done your work and may go play, unless you will fall out amongst yourselves."

It began soon enough. The Scots handed Charles over to Parliament in 1647. Parliament was divided against itself, its majority was Presbyterian but a powerful minority was Independent Puritan and this group, including Cromwell, was backed up by the Army. The matter of the "King's business" was hard to settle. First Parliament, then the Army, negotiated with Charles, who played for time. Parliament tried to disband the Army, but it refused to go. Cromwell showed his hand and seized the King from Parliament's keeping. On 31st May Charles was brought from Holdenby House in Northamptonshire to the Army camp at Newmarket. Now it was the Army's turn, but it could not agree either. The common soldiers had their own ideas of what to do with the King—"Get rid of him, proclaim a republic and give every man the vote." This sounds more like nineteenth- or twentieth-century talk and such strong democracy earned them the title of "Levellers". Cromwell and the officers had no stomach for such "rabble" talk and ordered the agitators back to their regiments.

Charles had been moved to Hampton Court, but he escaped from here in the November and fled to Carisbrooke Castle on

A Musketeer

68

the Isle of Wight. The King's sense of judgment was utterly wrong; he played a dangerous game and could not see how weak his position was. By the "Engagements" he struck a bargain with the Scots, that they would turn on their old allies and in return he would introduce Presbyterianism into England for three years and a new Church settlement would be worked out. Charles sealed his own fate. The divisions within the Army were forgotten. It met at a huge prayer meeting at Windsor and amidst tears of anger resolved "it was our duty if ever the Lord brought us back again in peace, to call Charles Stuart, that man of blood, to an account for that blood he had shed."

The war was a matter of months. The Scots invaded England in the summer of 1648 but got no farther than Warrington, and at Preston Cromwell thrashed a much larger Scottish army. Royalist support in England was weak, people chose to wait and see. The victory was the Army's and they were not going to make the mistake of 1645. They would settle the "King's business" for he had forfeited all right to negotiate, even all right to mercy.

The Presbyterian Parliament did not match the ruthless mood of the Army. It still wanted to come to terms with Charles. In December 1648 an Army detachment under Colonel Pride marched to Westminster, stopped all but fifty or sixty M.P.s from taking their seats and "purged" Parliament of its Presbyterians. The M.P.s left sitting became known as "The Rump".

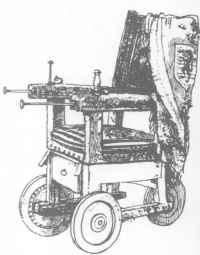

Fairfax's wheelchair

Parliament in 1651, from The Second Great Seal of the Commonwealth

69

The Execution of Charles I

The trial and execution of King Charles was more like a farce than a matter of life and death. The President of the Court, Bradshaw, had a bullet-proof hat. The members had a disguise of false beards and wigs. In the clamour for his blood Charles remained calm and regal, in marked contrast to Cromwell who behaved out of character by inking people's faces and throwing cushions in the air as he collected the death warrant signatures. Charles denied that the Court had any legal right and refused to answer the charges of "high treason against the nation". But no matter, he was condemned "a tyrant, traitor, murderer and public enemy" and sentenced to death. On 30th January, 1649, the King changed the farce into a tragedy. "Death is not terrible to me. I bless my God I am prepared," were his words before he walked to his execution. He stuck to his opinions: "A subject and a sovereign are clean different things"; and bowing his head to the axe's keen edge—he died. The sullen soldiers shouted in triumph but an eye-witness account reported: "The Blow I saw given and can truly say with a sad heart; at the instant whereof, I remember well, there was such a grone by the Thousands then present, as I never heard before and desire I may never hear again."

Cromwell
and Commonwealth

The end of the King did not end the causes of his death. England was a kingdom still divided against itself, and abroad the Stuart exiles determined to carry on the fight. It was easy to get rid of the head of the government but who should govern, and how, were questions still to be answered. From January 1649 to 1653 England was ruled by the "Rump" Parliament and a Council of State. This arrangement pleased few people other than the Rump. The new republic was surrounded by threats from Ireland, Scotland and Holland. There was little time to indulge in political arguments, the country needed to be defended.

Its defender was *Oliver Cromwell*. Times of crisis often produce men of genius who otherwise would have lived a very ordinary life. Cromwell did not become a soldier until he was forty-three. He came from the country gentry and was educated at Huntingdon and later at Sidney Sussex College, Cambridge. His roots seemed firmly set in that part of East Anglia, but in 1628 he became Member of Parliament for Huntingdon and in 1641 he represented Cambridge. It was during 1646 to 1649 that Cromwell really came to the fore as a soldier of renown and as a politician of sorts. The events of the next few years supported his military reputation and improved his political image. His name can still command either great love or great hate, and it is difficult to be detached when looking at the man; but one does not need to like him to recognise his greatness.

Oliver Cromwell

In Ireland, however, opinions of Cromwell are straightforward. He is still hated with deep bitterness and children are hushed to silence not with tales of "bogeymen" but threats of "Cromwell". He earned it, too, for although he could be a man of great humanity and tolerance, he had within him that overwhelming belief in the absolute rightness of his cause

71

Ireland in the sixteenth and seventeenth centuries

which makes monsters out of men, and of women, too, for there was the same quality in Mary Tudor and Catherine Medici. "I am persuaded that this is a righteous judgment of God upon these barbarous wretches," is his explanation of the sacking of Drogheda when 2000 men were slaughtered and of Wexford where the garrison met a similar fate. In nine months the Royalist threat in Ireland was effectively crushed and another chapter in England's exploitation of Ireland was written. Rebels were shipped to the West Indies, Irish lands were confiscated and given to English landlords and the seed of a deep hatred was sown.

Scotland, too, had rallied to the Stuart cause and proclaimed the young prince Charles II king. The new Charles was far removed from his father in character. Perhaps the Civil War had been a hard taskmaster, but he was more astute and less principled. He wanted his throne back and he would "sup with the Devil" to get it. In this case the "Devil" was a very saintly one—the Covenanters—and Charles had no qualms of conscience about signing the Covenant and becoming a true son of the "Kirk". Cromwell now had to face his old allies who believed as fervently as he that they were right and that God was with them. "I beseech you in the bowels of Christ, think it possible you may be mistaken," cautioned Cromwell and proceeded to prove it by defeating them at Dunbar. Charles pressed on, however, and invaded England, hoping for a lightning campaign and the capture of London. He marched through Lancashire and reached Worcester, where Cromwell caught up with him on 3rd September, 1651. The battle was a massacre, the Scots were tired and dispirited and they left behind 3000 dead and 10 000 prisoners. Charles managed to fly from the field and tradition has it that he saved himself by hiding in an oak tree. Oak Apple Day was later a Royalist holiday. The countryside was scoured for "a tall man about two yards high with hair a deep brown". A £1,000 reward was put on his head, but some Englishmen still loved their king and, disguised, he managed to reach Lyme Regis and take a boat for France.

On the high seas Robert Blake, a soldier turned sailor, was echoing Cromwell's successes. He chased Rupert's Royalist fleet out of Ireland and into the Mediterranean and another squadron persuaded the West Indies to drop their Royalist allegiance.

At the heart of the government, however, all was not well. The "Rump" was weak and Royalists and Presbyterians were at one in their hatred of the Rump. The Army had put it in power and the Army could remove it, which it did in 1653. Cromwell, hearing that it was trying to extend its power, marched to the House of Commons and, supported by a file of musketeers, ended its debate and its term of office. The Mace is the sign of Parliament's right to debate and Cromwell's famous, "What shall we do with that bauble? Take it away!" says more than he intended, for its going was the last act in the destruction of the traditional English government. King, Lords, and now Commons were no more, Cromwell and the Army remained.

The mace

Cromwell did not want to be a dictator and certainly not a king. He believed in the need of a Parliament to balance the power of a ruler, whatever his title, yet he dared not invite free elections. The mood of the majority of Englishmen of land was now anti-Puritan, and they would have brought back Charles II. Cromwell tried to solve his problem by keeping up the appearance of a Parliament. Congregational Churches were asked to submit the names of suitable M.P.s to a Council of Army Officers, who then chose 140 of them to represent Parliament. A leather seller from Fleet Street, one "Praise God Barebones" by name, has given this unusual Parliament his unusual name—the "Barebones Parliament". It met in July 1653 and ended in the December.

Government

England had never had written rules of government, i.e. a Constitution—custom and habit had shaped our government. In December 1653 the first written Constitution was drawn up as "The Instrument of Government". Oliver Cromwell was asked to become Lord Protector, and a Council of State and a Parliament were to share the powers of government. Sharing power is not easy; Charles I would say "Amen" to that, and Cromwell found it no easier. By January 1655, after sitting for only five months, Parliament was removed and, like Charles, he had to use personal rule.

England was now under undisguised military rule—the country, including Wales, was carved up into eleven districts, each placed under a Major-General and his troops. Cromwell ruled through them for over a year, and now that teeth had been given to the many Puritan Laws which had been passed since 1642, he sought to make people "godly". He aimed to "heal and settle" but like many before him and many to follow him, Cromwell could not realise that "virtue and godliness" cannot be compelled. Strict observation of the Sabbath, the banning of "plum pottage or nativity pies" at Christmas, the closing of theatres and bear-pits, and the outlawing of may-poles and football, did not endear his rule to ordinary folk.

73

John Bunyan

Stained-glass windows were destroyed, churches like Worcester Cathedral were used as stables and things of beauty treated like devices of the Devil.

It would be wrong, however, to think of the rule of the Puritans as a period of dismal gloom and that all Puritans were fanatics to the point of cruelty. They were honest, and sober. They respected justice and personal dignity and they understood love and family life. Men like the blind poet John Milton, the Bedfordshire tinker, John Bunyan, and the Quaker, George Fox, have enriched our history but their voices were heard after the Puritan rule. The pens of Puritan writers gave us more than the swords of Roundhead troopers.

England was no "godlier" in 1656 than she had been in 1654 and Cromwell tried to rule by consent once again and called his second Parliament. He had no more success than Charles and the Protector's answer to Parliamentary opposition was, "I do dissolve this Parliament, And let God be judge between you and me." Sixteen years of trouble had not solved

Cromwell dissolving the Long Parliament, 1653

England's problem when in 1658 a tired Cromwell put aside his strivings and died.

Utter confusion followed his death. His son "Tumbledown Dick", Richard Cromwell, became a reluctant and useless Lord Protector. The Rump was recalled and promptly quarrelled with the Army. It was left to one of the old guard, General Monk, to take action. He restored the Long Parliament by forcing the Rump to accept back the Presbyterians. Charles II saw his opportunity and from Breda in Holland set out his terms in the Declaration of Breda, promising forgiveness and "liberty to tender consciences". The Long Parliament disbanded and in the new elections Royalists were returned to Parliament.

May 27th, 1660, saw Charles II riding into London and the diarist John Evelyn tells us, "All was done without one drop of bloodshed and by that very army which rebelled against him . . . nor so joyful a day and so bright (was) ever seen in this nation." The bells rang, bonfires flared. The Earl of Clarendon gushed, "The King was attended through the City of London, where the streets were railed in on both sides, that the livery of all the companies of the City might appear with the more order and decency till he came to Whitehall, the windows all the way being full of ladies and persons of quality, who were impatient to fill their eyes with a beloved spectacle of which they had been so long deprived." On Tower Bridge the head of Oliver Cromwell grinned hideously from a spike, where it had been stuck for the occasion by triumphant Royalists.

Redcoats and Blue Jackets—The Commonwealth Abroad

The New Model Army wore scarlet uniforms and started the tradition of the British "redcoats" which lasted until the needs of modern warfare made khaki a more suitable fighting colour. English men-at-arms had not fared well in continental wars since the Middle Ages. Cromwell's troops, however, raised English prestige in Europe. The Commonwealth period, too, renewed England's naval power and made her sailors both respected and hated as they had not been since Elizabeth's days. By 1658 England was once more a European military and naval power.

The Commonwealth navy had conquered the island outposts of the royal cause. The Isle of Man and the Scilly Isles surrendered and in 1651 the New World Colonies were taken in hand. Virginia and Maryland on the American main-

George Fox

John Milton

The Art of War

A redcoat

75

Admiral Tromp

land, and Barbados, Bermuda and Antigua in the West Indies still supported the Stuart cause. The sight of a Parliamentarian naval squadron under Sir George Aysare soon changed Barbados' mind and Bermuda and Antigua followed suit. Virginia promised to be tougher but was not, and a single frigate was enough to persuade Maryland of the rightness of Parliament's cause.

In the seventeenth century, colonies were considered as existing for the convenience and wealth of the Mother Country. Nations looked upon each other as potential enemies. Trade was a means of strengthening yourself and weakening your rivals. England resented the Spanish control of South America but was just as jealous of her own colonial rights—"What is yours is mine, and what is mine is my own!" Royalist and Roundhead were in complete agreement on this point, if no other. "No peace beyond the line" was very real and though home governments were not at war, on the high seas English sailors were only too eager to have a go at French, Spanish, Dutch or the Devil himself.

Industry and Trade

It was the Dutch, however, who were our chief rivals. Outwardly England and the Netherlands had much in common—both were Puritan, after 1651 both were republics and both had been traditional allies against Spain. Both were sea powers, however, and rivals for trade. The Dutch resented the haughty English claims that Dutch ships should salute the English flag and that their fishing vessels could only fish the North Sea by paying toll to the English. In 1650 Parliament passed a law forbidding ships of other nations from entering colonial ports, and the famous Navigation Act a year later demanded that all trade with England should be in English ships, or ships from the country sending the goods. The Dutch were great "carriers" of other people's goods and this eventually hit them hard.

The Art of War

The Dutch Admiral Tromp and the English Admiral Blake exchanged shots off the coast of Kent in 1652 and started the First Dutch War. It lasted until 1654 and flared up again in Charles II's reign. The Battle of the Downs off Dungeness gave Tromp victory for he stopped Blake from hindering a convoy of merchantmen and sank six English warships, forcing Blake to retire to the shelter of the Downs. The story handed down is that he fastened a broom at his mast-head to show he had swept the English from the seas, but there does not appear to be much truth in the tale. If he had, though, he would soon have had to take it down—six months later Tromp was defeated off Dunkirk and the English blockaded the Dutch

76

coast. The climax came in July 1653 when Tromp fought his last battle off Texel. Twenty-six Dutch ships were sunk and 6000 men drowned, including the Dutch Admiral. England made a new name for herself as a sea power, but gained little more than glory.

Cromwell had never liked the Dutch war. He dreamed of a grand alliance of Protestant countries, dividing up the New World and the Far East between them and sharing the African trade. It is not so ridiculous when you know how Europe did this in the nineteenth century.

Admiral Blake

In 1653, however, the nearest it came to success was an expedition to the West Indies to teach the Spanish a lesson and break into the trade of the Spanish Main, a good old Elizabethan project. It was defeated when its ramshackle army tried to capture Hispaniola. The expedition's commander, General Venables, took Jamaica as a consolation prize. Rum, cricket and calypsos were to come much later and the early attempts to settle the new colony were shattered by disease.

It was like old times again, for England and Spain were soon at war, although this time England had France as an ally. On the high seas, Admiral Blake was successful, he blockaded Cadiz and destroyed a Spanish fleet at Santa Cruz. He died on board ship, however, as it sailed into Plymouth Sound in 1656. On the land the new redcoats fought well against the Spaniards, and at the Battle of the Dunes 6000 English soldiers won battle honours and captured Dunkirk. England now occupied a part of Europe for the first time since the loss of Calais, but it was of little use. In fact, the whole war was of little use. It was costly, and did nothing for England's life blood, her trade. Cromwell had seen that England's greatness would lie in her trade. He had a vision of the riches of the Americas and the Indies pouring into the Motherland in her own ships, and it was this dream which Charles II inherited and kept. The navy, trade and colonies, were to be England's sinews of greatness.

The Merrie Monarch

THE MERRIE MONARCH—CHARLES II (1660—85)

Charles II was thirty when he was restored to the throne. He was ruggedly handsome, bold in dress and manner and fond of pleasure, whether it was horse racing or the pursuit of pretty women. He was intelligent and dabbled in the new sciences, but he was also lazy and disliked the boredom of state affairs. Once his jester, Tom Killigrew, marched out of the court when Charles lazily refused to be concerned with State affairs. When asked where he was going Killigrew replied:

"To Hell to fetch Oliver Cromwell since his successor pays so little attention to the country's affairs."

Charles could match his jester wit for wit. When William Penn, the Quaker, refused to take off his hat in the King's presence Charles took off his own. "Friend Charles, why doest thou not keep on thy hat?" asked Penn. "'Tis the custom of this place that only one man should remain covered at a time."

Charles was an astute king. He had little feeling for religion and few principles, but he did understand people and he could make sense of his times. The clue to his actions lies in a remark he wrote to Sir Richard Bulstrode later in his reign. "I am weary of travelling and am resolved to go abroad no more." Charles had drifted around the courts of Europe for eleven years, and at times he was reduced to eating in taverns with a promise to pay later. It is not surprising that he was determined to keep his throne.

The bonfires and the cheers did not fool Charles. He knew that his return had solved nothing. Once the novelty had worn off the old bogeys would raise their heads again. Would Parliament be any more generous in providing money than earlier ones? Would they want to try to control his policies? How long would old religions and values lie quiet? But all this was in the future and in 1660 Charles was happy to live for

Charles II

the present. He was home and things looked good.

Charles had promised at Breda to let Parliament have a say in building "a peaceful and ordered settlement". A pardon was granted to the Crown's enemies "excepting only such persons as shall hereafter be excepted by Parliament". Only a few were executed—it might have been many more. "A liberty to tender consciences" in matters religious was promised, but Parliament was not as tolerant then, nor in the future, as their King and it never got down to dealing with it. The army had to be kept quiet and it was promised its back pay, which it received and was smartly disbanded, much to Parliament's relief. The thorny question of giving the King a workable income was tackled with good intentions. He was granted taxes, but no one knew how much government cost and squabbles were bound to come.

The Convention Parliament gave way to the Cavalier Parliament which was more Royalist than the King. Between 1661 and 1665 it passed a series of laws against Nonconformists. The Laws were called the Clarendon Code and named after Charles' chief minister, Lord Clarendon. Charles had no desire to hound the Nonconformists. His mother, Henrietta Maria, and his wife, Catherine of Braganza, were both Catholic. Furthermore, Charles had been helped after the Battle of Worcester by Catholic subjects, and if anything he leaned towards the Church of Rome. He sensed, however, the anti-Puritan passion which seethed in Parliament and sat back whilst the "Code" was shaped. The Corporation Act said that only members of the Church of England could be members of town corporations. The Act of Uniformity insisted upon the use of the Church of England Prayer Book. Behind these laws lay fear as well as religious prejudice. Parliament feared the old political strength of the Puritans, it wanted no more Cromwells. The attempt of Thomas Venner, a Quaker, to set up a monarchy of "King Jesus" in 1661 brought an hysterical attack upon Quakers throughout the land and 4000 were imprisoned. The Conventicle Act forbade the meeting of more than four people for a religious meeting other than Anglican, and the Five Mile Act stopped any Nonconformist minister from coming within five miles of a borough unless he promised not to try and alter the Church or the State.

The Clarendon Code kept the Nonconformists out of public life, but it did not crush them. It is not a coincidence that some of the best remembered names of Charles's reign were Nonconformists.

A Nonconformist preacher

John Bunyan, a Bedfordshire man and a Baptist, wrote *Pilgrim's Progress* whilst he was in Bedford Gaol for breaking the Clarendon Code. He spent about twelve years in prison.

John Milton was spared prison for he was no preacher, but he did have a deep religious faith. During the Commonwealth he was busy with politics and his pen defended the republic. He had become blind in 1651 but this did not stop his writing, and during Charles's reign he produced some of his best work, particularly "Paradise Lost" and "Samson Agonistes".

William Penn, the son of an admiral, who became a Quaker in his twenties, also spent time in prison. The Quakers were a kindly sect who believed in searching for inner peace and light, and were opposed to organised religion which seemed to insist unduly on outward show. Penn believed that "those who used force for religion could never be right" and worked for tolerance. He founded Pennsylvania in America in 1682 and its chief town, Philadelphia, means the City of Brotherly Love. His "Holy Experiment" of a state based on his religious beliefs failed, but his Quaker ideas did not and his dealings with the Red Indians were an object lesson in loving one's neighbour, which the rest of America would have done well to follow. Both Charles II and later James II respected Penn and like him would have welcomed tolerance in religion, although for different reasons. Charles did try to bring tolerance in the Declarations of Indulgence in 1662 and again in 1672, but the opposition was so strong that he dropped them. We shall see that his brother and heir, James II, had more religious feeling, but less political sense and he suffered for it.

William Penn

Plague, Fire and the Dutch

Questions of money or religion did not bother Charles unduly in 1665, but in the next two years even Providence seemed against him. England had to face a trio of perils, the Great Plague, the Great Fire and the Second Dutch War.

The Plague was nothing new, you will have come across it in the Black Death of 1348. Its true name was the bubonic plague, so called because its symptoms were hideous buboes which appeared on the joints. It had bedevilled Europe for centuries and it thrived in the dirt of narrow alleyways. From the spring of 1665 to the end of 1666 the Great Plague raged. We are lucky that three great diarists have given us accounts of the later Stuart period. They are Samuel Pepys, John Evelyn and Daniel Defoe.

In 1665 *Pepys* was a man about town and held an important

Samuel Pepys

Multituds flying from London by water in boats & barges.

Flying by land.

Burying the dead with a bell before them.   Searchers.

Carts full of dead to bury.

Carrying a corpse in a shroud

A dog-killer

Contemporary plague scenes

A doctor visits the sick

The City skyline before the Great Fire,

office as a clerk to the Navy Board. He frequented the taverns and coffee houses which abounded in London and like his royal master was a ladies' man. His diary tells us about the Court circle and society life.

John Evelyn was a scholar, a member of the Royal Society, a historian and a linguist. His diary is not as popular as Pepys's but is sensible and weighty.

Daniel Defoe hardly belongs to the reign of Charles II for he was only born in 1660 and did most of his writing at the end of the century. He was more of a journalist than a diarist, and famed for his "Robinson Crusoe". His "Journal of the Plague Year", however, is a vivid description of the period, even though it lacks the first-hand experience of either Pepys or Evelyn. He writes:

"The pain of the swelling was in particular very violent and to some intolerable; the physicians and surgeons may be said to have tortured many poor creatures even to death. . . . In some those swellings were made hard partly by the force of the distemper and partly by their being too violently drawn, and were so hard that no instrument could cut them and then they burnt them with caustics, so that many died raving mad with the torment."

Red crosses appeared on the doors of the stricken, with heart-rending pleas scrawled underneath, "Lord have mercy on us". Carts rumbled through the narrow streets with their ghastly load of dead. "Bring out your dead," called the driver, and added still more corpses to his load before carrying on his grisly way. The nobility panicked and fled from London, the ordinary people with little medical knowledge became resigned and relied upon superstitious cures. Huge fires were lit to drive

from the Swan Theatre to the Tower of London

away the plague, and sweet smelling herbs were sniffed at hopefully to kill the germs. It is strange how time eventually cures all, for our nursery rhyme "Ring-a-ring-a-roses" is really a plague song and the "roses" were not flowers but "boils", the "atishoo" the fever and the "all fall down" speaks for itself. People died and suffered; nearly 7000 died in one week alone, then a further calamity struck.

On 2nd September, 1666 (Lord's Day), Samuel Pepys noted:

"By and by Jane comes and tells me above three hundred houses have been burned down tonight by the fire we saw and that it is now burning down all Fish Street, by London Bridge."

John Evelyn wrote:

"The conflagration was so universal. The people so astonished that from the beginning, I know not by what despondency of fate, they hardly stirred to quench it, so that there was nothing heard or seen but crying and lamentation, running about like distracted creatures without at all attempting to save even their goods."

Pepys commented:

"Poor people staying in their houses so long till the fire touched them and then running into boats, or clambering from one pair of stairs by the water side to the other. And among other things the poor pigeons, I perceive, were loth to leave their houses, but hovered about the windows and balconies till they were, some of them, burned."

Old London had many closely packed wooden buildings which went up like tinder. Evelyn records: "For the heat with a long set of fair and warm weather had even ignited the air and prepared the materials to conceive the fire, which devoured

Building

83

Wren City church:
St Mary-le-bow
Building

Sir Christopher Wren

after an incredible manner houses, furniture and everything. . . . All the sky was of a fiery aspect, like the top of a burning oven and the light seen above 40 miles round about for many nights. God grant mine eyes may never behold the like, who now saw above 10,000 houses all in one flame; the noise and cracking and thunder of the impetuous flames, the shrieking of women and children, the hurry of people, the fall of towers, houses and churches was like a hideous storm."

The fire had started in Pudding Lane and eventually swallowed up St Paul's. The authorities could do nothing. Pepys tells us that the Lord Mayor found the situation too much for him—"At last met my Lord Mayor in Cannon Street, like a man spent, with a handkercher about his neck. To the King's message he cried, like a fainting woman, 'Lord, what can I do? I am spent, people will not obey me. I have been pulling down houses; but the fire overtakes us faster than we can do it.' That he needed no men soldiers; and that for himself he must go and refresh himself, having been up all night." Charles and his brother, James, behaved well and in the end the King directed the fire fighting himself. "It is not indeed imaginable how extraordinary the vigilance and activity of the King and Duke was, even labouring in person, and being present to command, order, reward, or encourage workmen, by which he showed his affection to his people and gained theirs."

Charles and the City authorities had to set about rebuilding London from the smouldering ruins. Many of the old landmarks had gone—St Paul's, Guildhall, the Royal Exchange and countless thousands of ordinary homes. In days before prefabricated buildings it is amazing that the houses were restored within five years. The rebuilding of public buildings took longer and in one sense was never completed for the plans of its master planner, *Christopher Wren*, were never carried out. His work is seen best in his churches. He built fifty in all, including St Paul's Cathedral, and his style of pillared belfries is easily recognised. Like many outstanding men of his day Wren was a man of many parts. He was a mathematician, astronomer and inventor as well as an architect.

The time of troubles was not ended by the fire for no sooner had the smoke drifted away than the thunder of Dutch guns resounded along the Thames. The Second Dutch War had started in 1664 and lasted until 1667. War was not hated as it is today, but was looked upon as a perfectly justifiable way of bringing wealth and glory to one's country. England deliberately looked for a fight. Sir Robert Holmes captured

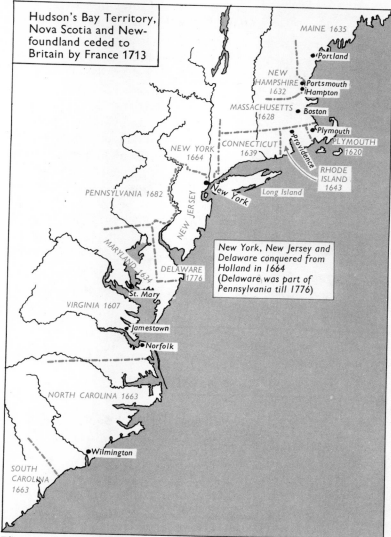

The colonisation of North America

Dutch trading posts in West Africa and Colonel Nicholls captured New Amsterdam in North America, soon to be renamed New York after the Duke of York. It was a key area for it linked up Virginia and New England.

The war was mainly a sea fight. It began with a resounding victory for the Duke of York off Lowestoft, but it ended with the Dutch cock-a-hoop. It was in the year of the Fire that Charles and his ministers decided to end the war, and to lay up the battle fleet in order to save money. This was foolish, for the Dutch were delighted to make the most of England's weakness. Dutch ships sailed up the Thames, crashed the boom which guarded Chatham harbour and after destroying four warships completed the humiliation by towing away the *Royal Charles*, the biggest ship of the time. Their guns could be heard at Bethnal Green and the London mob raved against the Admiralty and even against Charles. It helped to persuade the King that an early peace was needed. Louis XIV had already deserted the Dutch. The Treaty of Breda ended the war. The Dutch agreed to salute English ships in the Channel, but not on the high seas. England agreed that the Dutch could export to England goods they had imported from Germany. New Amsterdam stayed in English hands. Another Dutch War was still to be fought, but by 1667 the rivalry between the two nations was almost over.

Wars are always a costly business and the Dutch War raised the old question of royal finance. Parliament had voted the King money to fight the war and it demanded results. When it did not get them it howled for blood. Charles let his old minister and adviser, Lord Clarendon, suffer impeachment and exile as a scapegoat for plague, fire and war. He had to agree, too, that Parliament should inspect his accounts to see how the money had been spent. Charles I would have dissolved Parliament rather than do this, but Charles II chose to bend rather than to break.

Government

Louis XIV in the costume of Le Roi Soleil

Secret Councils, Secret Treaties and Secret Plots

Charles's later reign was not plagued by disease and fire, but by shortage of money and the religious fears of his people. It might almost be called the Age of Secrecy for he ruled for a time with the help of a secret council of five men, or a Cabal; the initials of their names spelt the word:

Clifford
Ashley
Buckingham
Arlington
Lauderdale

He made a secret alliance with Louis XIV and the country was scared out of its wits by rumours of a secret Popish plot.

Charles thought he could solve his money shortage and introduce religious tolerance by accepting money from His Most Catholic Majesty Louis XIV.

Louis XIV was the outstanding figure in Europe for sixty years and such grand titles as *"le grand monarque"* and *"le roi soleil"* came his way. Charles admired him greatly for he seemed to have everything Charles lacked—a secure throne,

Part of the Palace of Versailles

absolute power and plenty of money. He came to the throne in 1643 and died in 1715, and during this time he ruled completely. Versailles, his palace, reflected the splendour of His Majesty. French nobles flocked there. It had once been a small hunting lodge. Louis XIV spent a fortune on transforming it into a palace. The building was magnificent, so also Building were its formal terraces, gardens and fountains. The town of Versailles was replanned and great tree-lined avenues radiated from the palace. He dominated his neighbours and pushed France's boundaries wider and wider, to the Rhine in the north and to the Pyrenees in the south. It pleased him to befriend Charles in order to win him to the Catholic cause. In 1670 he was casting eyes on the Spanish Netherlands, which would bring France to the frontiers of Holland.

Charles and Louis hatched their plans at the Treaty of Dover (1670). It was really two treaties in one, a sham treaty and a secret one. The second was known only to a few trusted ministers. In it Charles agreed to declare war on the Dutch, when he would be joined by the French and announce that he had become a Roman Catholic, whilst Louis would pay Charles £166,000 and loan him 6000 troops. Between 1670 and 1678 Charles received £741,985 from Louis. He hoped that with Parliament out of the way the rest of the country might accept tolerance for non-Anglicans, and that a successful war against the old foe, Holland, might give him popularity and new power.

His first move was to provoke a war with the Dutch—"Our business is to break with them and yet lay the breach at their door," said Arlington. A supposed insult to the English fleet was thought up when the yacht *Merlin* sailed through a Dutch fleet and demanded a salute to which it had no right. The Third Dutch War began in 1672. The same year he made his second move and announced a Declaration of Indulgence, suspending the Clarendon Code and granting toleration to Puritans and Catholics alike.

The money Charles got from Louis would not provide for a long war. The odds were against the Dutch, but they stopped Louis on the land by cutting their dykes, and stopped Charles on the sea by the clever delaying tactics of Admiral de Ruyter. The young Prince William of Orange emerged as a cool leader and the Dutch rallied to him. Charles ran out of money and had to recall Parliament. Parliament's attitude was, "Withdraw the Indulgence and we will vote you money." The King had to agree. Parliament went one step further and passed the Test Act which kept all Nonconformists from holding office in the government or army, and then granted Charles £1,200,000. The new funds did not bring victory and in 1674 Charles deserted Louis and signed peace with Holland.

England was anxious about Charles and his Catholic sympathies. The Cabal broke up and James, the Duke of York, had to give up his office as Lord High Admiral because he was Catholic. The so-called Popish Plot shows how high feelings were running against the Catholics and against the King. At the centre of the intrigue were two peculiar characters, *Titus Oates* and *Israel Tonge*.

Oates was a plausible rogue, who had been expelled from school as a boy and from college as a young man. He had changed his faith twice from Anglican to Catholic and back again, and paraded a bogus degree from the University of Salamanca. Tonge really did have a degree from Oxford and earned his living by writing. They concocted a story which seems so ridiculous that it would not fool a half-wit. The Pope, the Jesuits and Louis IV had hatched a plot whereby a gang of thugs would assassinate Charles, take over London and put James, Duke of York, on the throne. The story was told in front of a magistrate, Sir Edmund Godfrey, who was found murdered some weeks later and this too was laid at the door of the Catholics. The whole thing was a cruel hoax, told for money, but behind it lay a little truth.

From 1678 to 1681 Roman Catholics were hounded. Thirty-five of them were executed on false charges, and even well-known figures like the Roman Catholic Bishop of Armagh were killed. Charles's words on hearing of the Bishop's trial show how his hopes of Catholic toleration, and perhaps his

Nell Gwyn

88

dreams of becoming Catholic, had been shattered—"I cannot pardon him because I dare not." Samuel Pepys was arrested during the Popish Plot hysteria.

Meanwhile Titus Oates lived like a lord and enjoyed his notoriety. A letter from Charles's chief minister Danby to Louis XIV asking for money was shown to Parliament. A howl went up for Danby's blood and Charles, seeing here a possible repetition of the impeachment of Lord Strafford in his father's reign, dissolved Parliament rather than surrender his minister.

Whigs, Tories and an Heir to the Throne

From 1678 Charles and his Parliaments quarrelled fiercely on who was to succeed him. Two parties emerged called the Whigs and the Tories. The Whigs were determined to stop James, Duke of York, from becoming king because he was a Catholic. Their leader, Lord Shaftesbury, wanted Charles's illegitimate son, the Duke of Monmouth, although others would have settled for Charles's daughter, Mary. Charles and the Tories stood by hereditary right and James. Three Parliaments were called and the question of succession was no nearer a solution. Charles found a solution, for the time being, by again accepting French money and getting rid of Parliament.

These were unhappy years and there were real fears of another civil war. The one lasting outcome of Charles's later Parliaments was the Habeas Corpus Amendment Act. An Englishman was given the right to demand by writ of habeas corpus that he should have his case examined by a court. This is a right denied to many European people, who can do nothing about wrongful arrest and imprisonment.

The King seemed more powerful during the last four years than in the previous twenty. The Rye House Plot showed, however, that silencing opposition in Parliament did not get rid of it in the country. A group of ex-Cromwellian officers were behind the scheme. Richard Rumbold, an old Roundhead, married to the widow of a maltster of Rye House, Hoddesdon, Hertfordshire, planned to use his home as a base for seizing the King and the Duke of York. The royal party usually rode from the races at Newmarket to London via a Roman road passing through Hoddesdon. It was here that they would be set upon. A fire at Newmarket speeded their departure and the plot misfired; one of the plotters sold out his comrades and heads rolled. The Duke of Monmouth was suspected, and Lord Russell and Algernon Sydney were arrested and executed.

Charles never did solve his quarrel with Parliament. On

6th February, 1685, Evelyn wrote in his diary:

"I went to London, hearing His Majesty had been the Monday before (February 2nd) surprised in his bed chamber with an apoplectic fit. . . . He still complained and was relapsing, often fainting, with sometimes epileptic symptoms till Wednesday, for which he was cupped, let blood in both jugulars, had both vomits and purges. . . . Thus he passed Thursday night with great difficulty, when complaining of a pain in his side, they drew 12 ounces more of blood from him . . . he lay dozing and after some conflict, the physicians despairing of him, he gave up the ghost at half an hour after eleven in the morning being the 6th February 1685 in the 26th year of his reign and 54th of his age." Evelyn did not mention that on his death-bed Charles was able to do something he had privately hoped to do for years. Father Huddleston, the Roman Catholic priest who had saved him after the Battle of Worcester, received him into the Catholic Church, too late to do political harm, soon enough to ease his conscience.

Charles II died on his own bed; a less able man might have followed his father to the scaffold, or died an exile's death as his brother James was to do.

James and
The Glorious Revolution

JAMES II (1685–88)

James's reign opened promisingly. The Tories were loyal to a man and his first Parliament was full of them. The Whigs still wanted a king firmly limited by Parliament, but many of them were merchants and James could expect their support for he had shown a keen interest in trade and colonies. Unfortunately, James was a typical Stuart. He was a man of honour and conviction, but he lacked political wisdom. He was stubborn to the point of stupidity. Above all he believed like James I and Charles I before him that he alone was right.

Titus Oates, of Popish Plot fame, soon discovered that James meant business for Titus was sentenced to life imprisonment, and received three thousand lashes. People were worried at the brutal way James had his revenge but the landing of the Duke of Monmouth soon diverted their minds.

James II

Titus Oates pilloried

Duke of Monmouth

Judge Jeffreys

Government

Monmouth's Rebellion

Less than a month after the first Parliament began, its meetings were interrupted by the landing of the Duke of Monmouth at Lyme Regis. Monmouth had fled to Holland when James became king, but he still hoped to be accepted as the legitimate heir to his father's throne. The rebellion was tragic from beginning to end. The Duke of Argyll was supposed to rouse the Highlands and Monmouth the West of England. The Scots would have none of Argyll and at the most Monmouth could only rally some 4000 foot soldiers and 500 horses—most of them through hunger rather than loyalty. He took his stand at Bridgwater in Somerset and a pitched battle was fought outside the town on Sedgemoor. Monmouth's raw troops fought well enough, but the Duke, seeing that the battle was hopeless, fled from the field. He was captured three days later, disguised and sleeping in a ditch in the New Forest.

The aftermath of Monmouth's Rebellion lost James more than his victory gained. In the heat of battle dreadful things are done. Certainly no one would have objected to Monmouth's execution, but the brutality of the reprisals shocked even James's friends. Lord Chief Justice Jeffreys sat in judgement in a series of "bloody" assizes. Three hundred rebels were hung and quartered, another 800 were shipped as slaves to the New World, many more were whipped, pilloried, branded and mutilated. The clock had been put back over a hundred years.

Catholic James

Monmouth's Rebellion meant that a large royal army could be formed. From a mere 6000 troops it grew to over 30000 encamped near London on Hounslow Heath. James insisted that he needed "a well-disciplined standing force", although the defeat of the rebellion had removed the need. He stupidly paraded his intentions by appointing Catholic officers and opening a Catholic chapel on the Heath. He misjudged the temper of his loyalist Parliament, however, when he asked them to accept his actions and repeal the Test Act, which allowed Anglicans alone to hold office. Parliament asked him to dismiss his officers and reduce the size of his army, James refused and Parliament was dismissed. James was thrown back on his personal government.

Englishmen did not need memories of personal rule to be frightened by James's actions. They had a living example under their noses, for Louis XIV of France, the most absolute

92

monarch in Europe, had recently turned on French Protestants, the Huguenots. He refused them their time-honoured freedom of worship and exiled their leaders. Thousands risked death to escape from France and many settled in England. James was no Louis but, even so, people reasoned that what an absolute monarch could do in France, a monarch without Parliament might do in England.

James tried to win the Nonconformists to his side by granting them religious toleration. He issued a Declaration of Indulgence freeing them and the Catholics from the Clarendon Code. The Nonconformists preferred to get their freedom from a Parliament and were not impressed. Tory Justices of the Peace, natural supporters of James, refused to apply the Indulgence. James was losing his friends.

A second Declaration was issued in 1688 and this time James tried to force it through and ordered that it should be read on two successive Sundays in every church in the land. Only seven churches in London obeyed. In Westminster Abbey most of the congregation walked out, Archbishop Sancroft of Canterbury and six other bishops petitioned the King to withdraw the Declaration. James reacted by calling the petition "a standard of rebellion" and arrested the bishops. They were put in the Tower and brought to trial. June 30th, 1688, was the fateful date in Stuart history for on this day the judges acquitted the bishops and all London rejoiced. James had challenged Parliament and the Church and had failed miserably. The tragedy was that James's actions sprang from honestly held beliefs and were directed against unjust and intolerant laws and a self-righteous Church. His motives, however, were as intolerant as those of his opponents and it took another 200 years for religious toleration to be accepted.

The seven bishops

The Glorious Revolution

The Whigs and Tories combined against James. Admiral Herbert, disguised as an ordinary seaman, carried a cautious message to William of Orange asking for his help. William landed in Tor Bay on 5th November, 1688. James considered offering some resistance but even he could see that the cause was lost. He smuggled his wife and son out of the country and tried to follow. He dropped the Great Seal, which was the sign of royal assent to Acts of Parliament, overboard in a puny gesture of defiance. Unfortunately for both James and William he was recognised as he sailed down the Thames and brought back to London. William had the commonsense to let him escape again and this time he succeeded in reaching France.

Government

93

William
and the last
of the Stuarts

William III

Government

WILLIAM (1689–1702), MARY (1689–94)
ANNE (1702–14)

William accepted the vacant throne for Dutch reasons, so that England's money and troops could help in the war with France. The Tories had joined with the Whigs to call in William, but it went against the grain for them to put someone on the throne who was not the direct heir to the throne. The Whigs alone were enthusiastic about the Revolution. It was a triumph for their belief that kings were appointed by men to provide good government; if their government was not good then men had the right to remove them.

The Convention Parliament which met in London in December 1688 drew up a Declaration of Rights, which later became the Bill of Rights. This document has become as important as the Magna Carta in English history, but because England does not have a written Constitution it is the way people have shaped our government in practice which is more important than any legal document.

The Bill of Rights was only a rough and ready list of conditions on which William and Mary would be offered the throne. Only a Protestant could become the ruler. The successors to the throne in the immediate future were to be the heirs of Mary, then Anne and finally any of William's heirs if Mary should die before him and he should remarry. It brought out and aired the views expressed earlier in the seventeenth century. Freedom of speech was essential in Parliament, and the king could not "suspend" or "dispense with" Parliament without its agreement. Elections were not to be tampered with, there was to be no standing army in peace-time without the agreement of Parliament, and the king was not to levy heavy fines.

The Toleration Act of 1689 was a typical middle of the way

94

The Lords and Commons presenting the Crown to William and Mary

agreement. It granted freedom of worship to all who accepted
basic Christian beliefs, who would declare against the Pope,
and who would acknowledge William as head of the English
Church. Protestant Nonconformists, known as Dissenters,
could have their own churches and schools. Their position
improved in other ways, for although they were still debarred
from public life many of them found a way round by occasionally conforming to the Church of England by attending
church once a year. More important than Acts of Parliament
was the attitude of tolerance which men were beginning to
learn at long last.

The growing spirit of tolerance helped the Catholics too.
Their lot was worsened on paper, for they were forbidden to
carry arms or to own a horse worth more than five pounds, or
to live in London and Westminster. These measures were

Mary II

The Art of War

intended to check any political or military threat from them, similar to the happenings of James's reign. In practice, they were allowed to worship quietly and they were happily freed from the taint of treason which had been with them from the days of Queen Elizabeth.

King William's War

By the spring of 1689 Englishmen had more to occupy their minds than Acts of Parliament.

In May the treaty of the Grand Alliance was signed in Vienna by "Dutch" William and later by him as King of England. Along with Holland, Austria, and certain German States (soon to be joined by Spain and Savoy), England was committed to war with France. This has been called "King William's War", hinting that England was dragged into it by Dutch interests. William certainly wanted English help in his Dutch interests, but when Louis XIV took up James II's cause, and when he threatened the Low Countries as part of his dream of a French Empire in Europe, he made it an English war. England could never be happy with a strong power in control of the Low Countries.

At first glance it seems as though Louis had over-reached himself. England and Holland were the two strongest sea powers in Europe, whilst Austria, Germany and Spain virtually surrounded France. You must remember, however, that the Austrian Empire was big but weak, whilst the German states were a host of small powers and not the united nation of the nineteenth and twentieth centuries. Spain had ceased to be a great power. Louis' plan of pushing France's boundaries to the Rhine in the east and north, and of crossing the Pyrenees in the south, was not so foolish as it might seem.

The struggle against France appears to be two wars. The first lasted from 1689 to 1697 when it was ended by the Treaty of Ryswick. The second, known as the War of Spanish Succession, began in 1701 and lasted until the Treaty of Utrecht in 1713. If we take a still longer view the wars with France lasted until 1815, for just as Spain was England's rival in the sixteenth century and the Dutch in the seventeenth century, so France became our enemy in the eighteenth century. By this time warfare had become more than a fight between single nations. It was fought across Europe, large numbers of troops were used and it was very costly. The war which started in 1689 was in many ways the first modern war.

In the early stages of the struggle Englishmen were not so

much interested in the wider struggle in Europe; they were concerned with keeping the English Government firm against James II's attempts to regain his throne with French help. There were two possible points of attack by James, either Scotland or Ireland. In Scotland the Lowlanders welcomed William as king, and used the Revolution to overthrow their hated bishops and to restore the Presbyterian churches, the Scottish "kirks".

In the Highlands, however, the clansmen were Catholic and stayed true to James. Their leader was *Claverhouse, Viscount Dundee*, known in the Scottish ballad as "Bonnie Dundee". He led a Highland force at Killicrankie against a Lowland army commanded by General Mackay. He forced Mackay to retreat, but was killed in the battle and his death ended Highland hopes. A second chance came James's way in 1692 with the Massacre of Glencoe. This piece of treachery roused the Highlands to fury and has caught people's imagination ever since. The clansmen were required to sign an oath to the new sovereigns William and Mary by New Year's Day 1692. Macdonald of Glencoe arrived at Fort William too late and this was used by his enemies as an excuse to get rid of him and his troublesome clansmen. King William signed the paper of execution, and it has been argued ever since as to whether or not he knew what he was signing. The troops at Fort William, most of them Campbells of the Duke of Argyll's regiment, were given the job to do. It was the way they carried out their task which has made Glencoe such a household word. A hundred of them were treated as guests by the Macdonalds for over a week, then during one night the Campbells attacked their hosts. Macdonald of Glencoe was murdered and with him thirty-three men, two women and two children. The rest escaped to tell the tale of treachery, but there was no call to arms.

James made his last attempt to recapture his throne in Ireland. Tyrconnel had kept Ireland true to James and within three months of his flight from London James was on Irish soil. His Catholic faith was his greatest asset there, for the Catholic Irish had been persecuted for a century by Protestant England. Her trade was subdued by English merchants and her land confiscated and given to English landowners. The Protestant Irish were stronger in Ulster and they concentrated on Enniskillen and Londonderry. James's Irish troops besieged these places, but failed to take them. A year elapsed, and in June 1690 William himself landed in Ireland. James took up his position north of Dublin on the River Boyne. On the banks

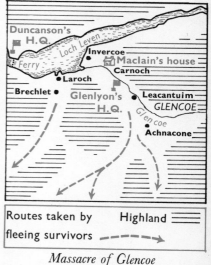

Routes taken by fleeing survivors ------→   Highland =====

Massacre of Glencoe

Agriculture

G

of this Irish river the English throne was lost for ever to James Stuart and his heirs.

James fled once more to France. Catholics could not buy land or educate their children in their faith. The Irish peasant paid his tithe to a Protestant English Church. Irish trade was ruined in the interests of England, cattle could not be exported and their linen could only be exported to England. Ireland stayed crushed for another hundred years.

In these early years of the war there was a very real threat of a French invasion. Louis planned to get control of the Channel and land troops in southern England. The sea war was as important in 1690 as the air war in the Battle of Britain in 1940. The French defeated Admiral Herbert off Beachy Head, but did not take advantage of their victory. Probably because the English fleet had stayed intact, the invasion was delayed for another year. James II joined the waiting forces and England waited as she had at the time of the Armada. This time the Dutch and English fleets outnumbered the French by more than two to one and they gained a resounding victory at La Hogue. The French fleet did not recover from this defeat for the rest of the war.

The real centre of the war in Europe was Flanders. This strip of land separated France and Holland. Its rivers and highways were controlled by a series of forts like Namur, Liège and Mons and the fighting there was a bloody, dreary business of sieges and trenches. William raised England's army from 35 000 to 90 000, but it was ill-prepared for a European war and although William was as brave as a lion he was not a great military leader. From 1690 to 1694 the war went badly. The French general, the Duke of Luxembourg, captured fortress after fortress. In Germany, Hungary and Spain the allies fared no better.

The year 1695 proved the turning-point of the war and, strangely enough, the reason why William did better was not mainly military. In 1694 it had become obvious that the war was so costly that it could not be paid for by the usual methods of raising taxes through Parliament. The total cost of the war was £40,000,000 and some of this money had to be met out of credit. The Bank of England got its Charter of Incorporation in 1694, and undertook to loan the Government £1,200,000 at 8 per cent. In return the bank received privileges such as the right to issue notes, and to conduct much government business.

William now found that he had money to equip his forces, and businessmen found that it was in their interests to keep William on the throne. In 1695 the French surrendered Namur to William's troops and Louis found that despite his other victories the war was proving costly. He had his eye, too, on a bigger "plum"—the whole of Spain and her empire. He agreed to the Treaty of Ryswick in 1697. Holland was safe from the French, and the English throne was safe from James Stuart, despite Mary's death in 1694.

The War of Spanish Succession

The years 1697 to 1701 hardly earn the title of peace, for peace is not only an absence of war, but the existence of co-operation between nations. In these troubled years the nations were brewing more trouble. Charles II of Spain was dying slowly and there was no one person to succeed him. The Hapsburg rulers of Austria had a claim in Archduke Charles. The Prince of Bavaria was another possibility and so was one of the French Bourbon princes. Europe could never be happy if Austria and Spain were once again united as they had been in Tudor days, when Charles V had ruled the Hapsburg lands. France would have suffered particularly. Holland and England calmly agreed, therefore, to divide up the Spanish lands in two Partition Treaties. Charles II himself, however, took a hand in saying what should happen to his own lands, and he left all of them in his will to Philip of Anjou, the grandson of Louis, provided the two crowns were not united. This delighted Louis, the Partition Treaties were forgotten and he accepted the will when Charles died in 1700. Holland and England might have accepted it too if Louis' ambition had not overwhelmed his common sense. He attacked the Flanders forts. He closed French and Spanish ports to English and Dutch ships and he proclaimed James II's son, James Edward, as James III of England. Europe was back to square one; the Grand Alliance was renewed in 1701. William did not take any part in the new struggle for he died in 1702. *Queen Anne*. another daughter of James II and sister of Mary, became the sole ruler. It was as well for England that Anne's great friend at this time was Sarah Churchill, wife of John Churchill, Earl of Marlborough, for Marlborough and the War of Spanish Succession go hand-in-hand in English history.

John Churchill was the son of a minor politician who made his name and his fortune slowly but thoroughly. He was a handsome man and he married a beauty of the day, Sarah Jennings. He would probably have made a reputation without the help of a clever wife for he had a cool, calculating mind and he let it rule his heart. He had plenty of courage and

Sarah Churchill

Queen Anne

99

John Churchill

The Art of War

became an excellent soldier and tactician. He learned his trade over thirty years, first at sea under James, Duke of York, and later with a famous French general, Turenne, when he fought against the Dutch in 1673. It was as the ally of the Dutch, however, that he made his name. He had no great interest in politics and considered parties "unreasonable and unjust". His own leanings were towards the Tories, but he became a Whig when it suited him. His career was not all plain sailing, for he lost the favour of William in 1692 and with it lost all his offices. He spent six weeks in the Tower and was in disgrace for three years. His great victories in the War of Spanish Succession gave him an unrivalled position. The magnificence of Blenheim Palace will give you some idea just how lofty his position was. A fickle nation, however, saw him go into voluntary exile in 1712 when he lost the confidence of the Queen and when the gleeful Tories trumped up charges of corruption against him. He did not return to England until Anne's death in 1714 and he died himself in 1722. His family fortunes have, of course, continued to the present day.

We must be satisfied with a glimpse of the career of Marl-borough in the Spanish Succession War. In an age when warfare was a very formal affair, fought according to the book of rules, Marlborough brought a breath of fresh air and fresh tactics. His basic idea was that attack was the best form of defence. In 1704 he marched his mixed army of Dutch,

Blenheim Palace

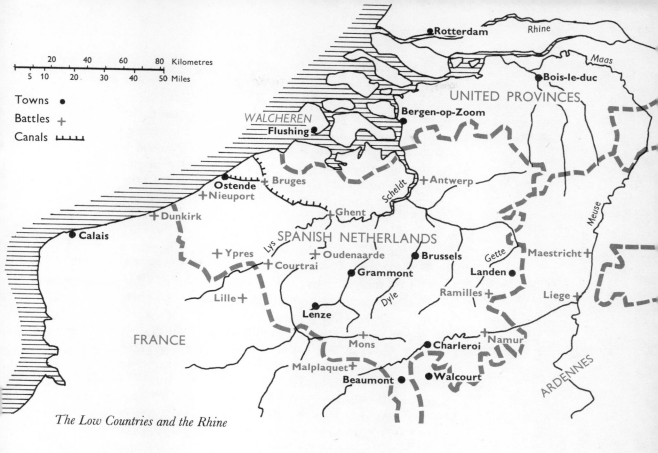

The Low Countries and the Rhine

German and English troops from the Netherlands, across Germany, and defeated the French at Blenheim. This was Louis XIV's first great defeat in battle and it was probably Marlborough's greatest victory. It was not his last, for between 1704 and 1709 they read like the British army's regimental honours list—*Ramillies* (1706), *Oudenarde* (1708), *Malplaquet* (1709). Even these fell short of his hopes, however, for he had wanted to attack Paris but he could not persuade the allies, particularly the defensive-minded Dutch, into such a bold venture. He had to be content with a slow opening of the way towards Paris by seizing first one fortress and then another.

Louis did not fare any better in the other theatres of war than he had in Germany and the Netherlands. The English captured Gibraltar from Spain and the Austrian commander Eugene defeated the French in Italy. By 1708 Louis was ready for peace but the Austrian Emperor was not, nor were the English Whigs. They wanted to beat France to her knees. They underestimated their enemy and Louis chose to fight on. By 1710 England was tired of war and Anne dismissed the Whig war leaders and called in the Tories to make a separate peace.

The ending of the war was a slow business; the Treaty of Utrecht was not signed until 1713. The main results were that England gained Nova Scotia, Hudson Bay, Newfoundland, Gibraltar and Minorca. The French dropped their support of James Edward and the Spaniards opened up trade to English merchants in South America. In particular the slave trade with the Americas became almost entirely English. Austria gained lands in the Netherlands and Italy, whilst the Bourbons kept the Spanish throne with Philip of Anjou as king as, of course, had been originally intended in Charles II's will.

Industry and Trade

Whigs and Tories again and another vacant throne

The Treaty of Utrecht was a Tory peace but this was not to their advantage at home. They had deserted their allies and one of them, George of Hanover, was likely to be the next King of England. It was obvious from 1700 that Queen Anne would have no heir to the throne. She had eighteen children but the last of them, William, had died in 1700 at the age of eleven. The Act of Settlement tried to prevent trouble by settling the throne on the Electress Sophia of Hanover or her heirs, but there was always the fear of another civil war as long as the Stuart exiles were alive.

James Edward, better known as the "Old Pretender", carried on his father's hope of one day returning to England. He tried a comeback in 1708, basing his hopes on the Scottish Jacobites. Jacobite comes from the Latin for "James" and they were strongest in Scotland. In 1707 the Act of Union had joined the Scottish and English Parliaments. You will remember that the crowns had been united since 1603. Forty-five Scottish M.P.s went to the House of Commons at Westminster and sixteen peers joined the House of Lords. Scotland could now share in England's trading wealth and colonial empire. The Scottish Parliament ceased to exist, however, and many Scots resented the Union and still do. James planned to land in Scotland but the English secret service discovered the plot and he was headed off in the Firth of Forth.

Government

Many English Tories favoured the "King over the water" in their hearts. James Edward, however, was a devout Roman Catholic and this was the stumbling block for the Tories. They feared the death of Anne and the coming of George of Hanover, but they could not support a Catholic king. In the last three years of Anne's reign two men were rivals for the leadership of the Tories. The moderate Robert Harley, Lord Oxford, had got them back into power in 1710 and realised that the Jacobite

The 'Old Pretender'

102

cause was weak. Viscount Bolingbroke was a "die-hard" and was willing to toy with the Jacobites if it would keep them in power. He took over from Oxford and approached James Edward, offering him support if he would change his faith. James would not and Bolingbroke and the Tories were suspected of Jacobite sympathies. As Anne lay dying she turned against them and Bolingbroke fled to Europe. It was now certain that George of Hanover would soon be George I of England and that his friends, the Whigs, would once again become a power in the land.

The end of an era

The death of Anne in 1714 brought an era to its close. The happy restoration of the Stuarts in 1660 had come to nothing after all. The long struggle between the Stuarts and their parliaments ended in Parliament's favour. But all had not been strife. In the years since 1660 England had flourished. Her trade with the New World and the Indies had grown. She had become the mistress of the west coast of North America and the East India Company was a power in the East. The Royal Navy had won control of the English Channel and had a footing in the Mediterranean. The Spanish Main was now more English than Spanish.

Industry and Trade

England was building up her industries, too, ready for a leap forward in the next century into the Industrial Revolution. The clothing industry in the West Riding of Yorkshire and East Anglia flourished on war demands; so did the iron and ship-building industries. The immigrants from Europe, particularly the French Huguenots, brought new skills in silk weaving, paper-making and cutlery and these new industries were large-scale and were often controlled by capitalists, i.e. men who invested money in industry. This was the shape of things to come.

The arts flourished, for art needs money to be patronised. This period was one of the greatest in English architecture. London was rebuilt, aristocratic palaces like Blenheim and Castle Howard were built on classical lines. English life benefitted artistically by our close contacts with Europe. Architects such as Vanbrugh and Wren, and the wood-carver Grinling Gibbons, were men with European reputations. Painting did not reach so high a standard. Portrait painting was popular, as you would expect in an aristocratic age, and here it was a German, Godfrey Kneller, and a Swede, Michael Dahl, who were best known. Music was given a rebirth after

Building

The Arts

Carved panels in St. Paul's Cathedral

Sir Isaac Newton

the Puritan years and Henry Purcell was one of England's greatest musicians, although he was temporarily overshadowed by the German, George Frederick Handel, who first visited London in 1706. The theatre was boosted by the Restoration and for a time ran riot in crude, witty comedies. William Congreve was the best of the English dramatists but again much was borrowed from French playwrights, like Molière. In literature writers abounded and many of their works still gladden the ears of English children. Pope, Dryden, Milton, Defoe and Swift are household names in English literature. Last but by no means least this was the age of scientific thinking. Charles II himself belonged to the Royal Society. Alexander Pope might poke fun at Sir Isaac Newton with his

> "Nature and Nature's Law lay hid in night,
>   God said, Let Newton be! And all was light",

Ideas

but Newton is the father figure of English mathematics, physics and astronomy. Some of you have probably learned Boyle's Law by heart. Robert Boyle was one of the pioneers of physics and chemistry. The later Stuarts left a rich heritage to their German successors.

104

THE SECTIONS

Agriculture

A man using a trenching spade

The discoveries of new lands in the fifteenth and sixteenth centuries led to many new products entering Europe. Some, such as potatoes, maize and rice, could be grown in Europe; others were imported in ever-increasing quantities. The potato became an important food in many countries, particularly Ireland.

The popularity of tea, coffee and cocoa led to an increase in the imports of these products, and an increase in the consumption of sugar. The liking for sweet puddings also led to more sugar being eaten. Tobacco, whether chewed, smoked or taken as snuff, also grew in popularity during this period. The turkey was brought to England from Mexico in the sixteenth century and became a favourite dish for Christmas dinner a century later.

The fifteenth and sixteenth centuries brought marked changes in the economic and social life of English people, many of which resulted from changes in farming and land ownership. If you look at advertisements of houses for sale in the paper, you will see the words "freehold" and "leasehold" mentioned frequently. A freeholder has clear title to his property and he and his descendants can occupy it for ever if they wish. A leaseholder pays a ground rent and can only occupy his property for a given number of years. In other words, the land is leased to him.

As the feudal system broke up, many villeins became what was known as copy holders. The terms of their tenancy were kept by the manor bailiff on the roll of the manor court and they were given a copy themselves, hence the word copyholder. Some copyholders got clear terms from the lord for their tenancy, while others got vague terms, where much was left to the discretion of the lord. For instance, when a copyholder died, his son had to make some payment or gift to the lord so as to inherit the land. If a lord wished to get rid of a tenant, then at such a time all he had to do was to ask for a very large payment or gift. If the son could not pay the lord could take the land. So whether you were a leaseholder in the twentieth century or a copyholder in the sixteenth century, you did not enjoy the privileges of a freeholder.

The barons of the Middle Ages valued their estates partly for the number of soldiers they provided. The landlord of Tudor times valued his estates largely for the amount of rent they brought in. The Tudor landlord was, in many cases, a man who bought land and farmed it to make a profit, and one profitable type of farming was the rearing of sheep. Sheep were likened to caterpillars by some writers, eating the livelihood of many villages as lords turned the land from ploughland to pasture, and from common to private field.

Farms grew bigger and fewer men were needed and as early as 1489 Henry VII's government passed two acts to try to stop land being enclosed for private gain. The first expressed the fear that the Isle of Wight might lose so many people as to be defenceless against an invasion. Although they tried, none of the Tudor kings or queens succeeded in stopping the enclosure of land or the desertion of villages. We may feel sympathy for the villagers, who in some cases were forced to become beggars, but we must remember that without enclosures improvements could not so easily have taken place. As Thomas Tusser, a quick-witted Suffolk man, wrote:
"Where cattle may run about roving at will
From pasture to pasture poor belly to fill
These pasture and cattle both hungry and bare
For want of good husbandry worser do fare."

Enclosure of land and an increase of sheep farming went hand in hand. Unfortunately, since sixteenth-century farmers did not know of the value of clover and root crops such as turnips and mangolds, mixed farming could not take place. Until these crops were grown English farmers could not experience the truth of the saying that the foot of the sheep turns sand into gold.

FARM IMPLEMENTS 1500–1700
There were not many changes in the types of farm tools used during this period. The changes which did take place were in design and in the materials used for making the tools. The spade in the illustration cut turf and dug a trench and was used in drainage work. The finished trench was filled with brushwood and stone and helped considerably in draining fields. This was necessary for both pasture and arable land.

On the other hand some farmers in Tudor times, rather like the Ancient Egyptians, realised that flooding could be an advantage. In some parts of England, for instance near Worcester, water-meadows were constructed which gave heavy yields of feed for cattle. Whether it was water-meadows or sheep closes, these improvements were difficult without enclosure.

Water-meadows at Worcester

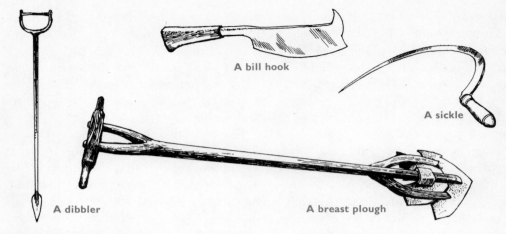

A bill hook

A sickle

A dibbler

A breast plough

Agricultural implements

The sowing of seed was still done by the method of broadcasting; for large seeds such as beans a dibbler was used. This was about one metre long and had a handle like a spade. A man made the holes with the dibbler while the women and children followed, dropping the beans into the holes. Sickles, hooks and scythes were used at harvest time, and threshing was done with a flail.

THE DRAINING OF THE FENS

Before Cornelis Vermuyden started his scheme to drain the fens, this area of some 300 000 hectares was the home of the fenmen. The marshes were to them what the commons and wastelands were to the villagers in other parts of the country. Geese and other waterfowl and fish were to be had in plenty, and the men of the fens resented the attempt to drain the land for it meant an end to their way of life. They destroyed many of the embankments, set fire to the mills, filled up drains and attacked the workmen. Some verses of these fenmen survive, one says:

Come brethren of the water, and let us all assemble,
To treat upon this matter which makes us quake and tremble,
For we shall rue it, if't be true, the Fens be undertaken,
And where we feed in fen and reed, they'll feed both beef and bacon.

As in the case of enclosure for sheep farming someone was going to lose, and the fenmen did their best to stop Vermuyden's plans being put into effect.

Humphrey Bradley was the first to put forward a clear-cut scheme to drain a large area of the fens. But it was not until some fifty years later that Vermuyden

Map of the Fenlands, position of the Bedford Level

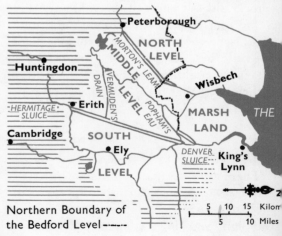

Northern Boundary of the Bedford Level ------

completed the task of reclaiming some 120 000 hectares of fenland. This area equals seven-tenths of the area reclaimed in the Netherlands between 1540 and 1690! Vermuyden's scheme was a good one, but he left one important point out of his calculations. He used the methods of his native Netherlands, methods not used by English engineers at this time. The water was removed from the fens by drainage and was controlled by new embankments and dams. Once the water was drained away the peaty land began to shrink and the land surface dropped. As the land dropped the drainage schemes became less and less effective and by 1664 schemes were put forward to drain the land by pumps driven by windmills.

FARMING IN IRELAND, SCOTLAND AND WALES

The unions with Wales and Scotland, and the Elizabethan conquest of Ireland took place during the centuries covered by this book. The first of the unions, that with Wales in 1536, was the most successful, whilst the conquest of Ireland brought little but strife and eventually disaster in the form of the terrible famine of 1844–45. The fortunes of Scotland lay somewhere between the experiences of the other two.

Ireland

Macaulay called Ireland "that vast expanse of emerald meadow saturated by the moisture of the Atlantic". Most of the Irish were pasture farmers moving with their herds and building temporary huts with branches of trees and sods of earth. The part of Ireland under English rule was the Pale and here some English customs were taken up by the Irish. Some Irish Palesmen had even taken to the English custom of washing their shirt four

or five times a year!

Beyond the Pale life was primitive; there was no harness for horses to pull ploughs, they were tied by their tails to the cross bar of a small plough. In battle the Irishman used the spear in a backhanded manner to reduce the risk of being thrown from his mount as he had no stirrup. The English regarded Ireland as a colony and in Northern Ireland a determined attempt was made from the sixteenth century to the reign of William III to turn the North-east into a Protestant colony. This meant that much of the land fell into the hands of English landlords.

By the eighteenth century the Irish tenants were very badly off. They lived in mud cabins, went barefooted and in rags and their main food was potatoes and milk. The rest of this grim story is dealt with in Book 3.

Scotland

Much of Scotland was mountain, moor, heath and watery waste. It was a difficult land for the farmer and the system used to combat the difficulties was known as runrig. The men of a village divided the land into the infield and the outfield. The infield, the best land lying near to the village, was manured and kept in constant cultivation. The outfield, the poorer land, was occasionally farmed, for several years, before it was given a long rest which could be for over ten years.

The Scottish plough was heavy and cumbersome and the villagers had to club together to provide enough beasts to make up a plough team. Eight or more oxen were needed and the land was ploughed into ridges. This was the only method of draining the land. The main crops grown were oats and barley.

The farmhouses were made of undressed stones with divots of earth between them

Agriculture

to keep the weather out. A rough framework of boughs rested on the rafters and a thatch of rushes, fern or heather was fastened down with straw ropes. A gap in the side wall performed two duties: it let the smoke out and let the light in. Robert Burns described such a place in his poem *The Vision*:

> There, lanely by the ingle-check
> I sat and ey's the spewing reek,
> That fill'd wi' hoast-provoking smeek
> The auld clay biggin;
> Ah' heard the restless rattons squeak
> About the riggin'.

The peasants of Scotland led a very hard life and in some years there was famine.

Wales

Wales was brought under English rule after Edward I defeated Llewellyn. It was unified with England in 1536 and this union left few of the bitter memories associated with the later English unions with Scotland and with Ireland. Before the union the English settlers occupied the low-lying more fertile ground and cultivated it on a system similar to that used on English manors. The Welsh herdsmen lived in the hills, but their Celtic laws and customs largely disappeared after the union. By the later sixteenth century most farms were held on yearly tenancies from landowners who adopted English speech and manners.

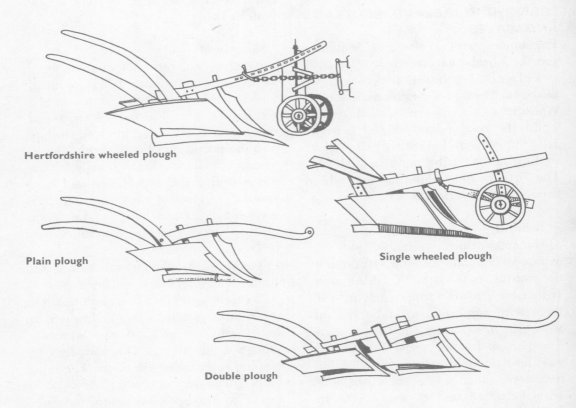

Hertfordshire wheeled plough

Plain plough

Single wheeled plough

Double plough

Seventeenth-century ploughs

Building and Town Planning

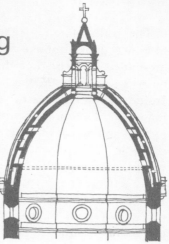

The construction of the dome

The castle of the Middle Ages was built to give its occupiers security, for in some countries kings and princes were weak and unable to extend the king's peace to all parts of the realm. During the sixteenth and seventeenth centuries, government in many parts of Europe was stronger and as a result there was less chance of internal strife. In these later centuries men did not have to worry so much about defence, therefore their houses could be spacious, light and well decorated. It was in Italy that the Gothic architecture of the Middle Ages was replaced by a new style, partly based on a study of the architecture of Ancient Rome. The changes made in Italy in the fifteenth century were followed by similar changes in other European countries. In England the full effects of the changes in design and building construction were not felt until the seventeenth century.

The buildings of the Middle Ages were constructed to meet the needs of soldiers and priests, but those of fifteenth-century Italy were often designed for merchants and bankers. These worldly men wanted houses which were beautiful, spacious and very different from buildings which would meet the needs of a bishop or noble of the Middle Ages.

Brunelleschi (1377–1446), although a goldsmith by training, was an architect of genius. The dome of the cathedral at Florence was a superb example of his work.

The dome of the Cathedral at Florence

H

Building

The walls of many of the palaces in Florence look immensely strong to a present-day tourist, but the stone blocks he sees are no more than a thin facing. Inside, the wall is made of brick and rubble masonry. The boldness of Renaissance men is reflected in their building, for example the projecting cornice. This would often overhang the streets by over two metres. The cornice on the Strozzi Palace overhung by 220 centimetres. This was achieved by increasing the thickness of the wall as shown in the diagram.

The timber frame of a 16th-century house

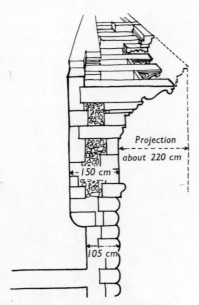

Cross-section of wall of Strozzi Palace

A Tudor house was built differently from a modern house. Instead of the wood arriving at the site ready sawn for use, the Tudor carpenter had often to fell the trees and saw them up by hand. The oaks were sawn over a pit; the man at the top being the "top sawyer", the one in the pit the "bottom sawyer". Smaller pieces of wood were squared up with an adze, the sixteenth-century equivalent of a plane. A man using an adze stood over the wood

taking off thick shavings. Floors surfaced in this way, when polished and caught in the sunlight, have an unusual and pleasant, dimpled effect. If we follow through the building of a timber framed house we can appreciate its special features.

Bricks were used for the foundations to keep the wood away from the damp earth. On top of the brickwork a wooden sill piece was laid and into this the studs were framed. Another sill was laid on top of the studs and formed the support for the joists which were to carry the next floor. The joists jutted out beyond the sills and as a result every floor was larger in area than the one below it, and seen from the outside these houses seemed to overhang the street.

The ends of the joists were covered by barge boards which were often beautifully carved. As timber grew scarce in later Tudor and Stuart times fewer studs were used and the spaces between them were filled by brick instead of wattle and

An adze

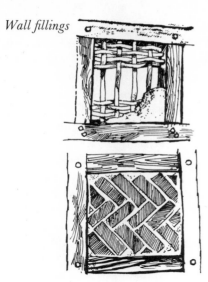

Wall fillings

stone and it was then split open. The stone "slates" were not bedded in mortar, but were laid dry with oak pegs driven into them to keep them in place. True slates were split in a similar way and were used in the South-west and the North-west. In many areas thatch made from straw was used; but in places where reeds were available they were used to make very long-lasting roofs.

The other new features which you could see from the outside of a Tudor house were chimneys and glass windows. Many chimneys had patterns on them, such as those on Wolsey's palace at Hampton Court.

Hampton Court Palace

daub. Wattle and daub was a wooden framework made of hazel or brushwood plastered over by clay. In East Anglia the outside wall was often plastered. In addition, patterns were scratched in the plaster with a comb; this was known as pargetting.

Pargetting patterns

There were as many different roofing materials used as there were differences in walls. In the Cotswolds and the Pennines stone roofing was used. The stone was chosen and left out in the winter frosts. This loosened the natural layers of the

Building

▲ *Hardwick Hall, Derbyshire*
▼ *The Great Staircase at Hatfield House, Hertfordshire*

Large amounts of glass were used in the windows of great houses such as Hardwick Hall. Lord Bacon complained that "You shall have sometimes fair houses so full of glass, that one cannot tell where to be come, to be out of the sun or cold."

Inside the houses, wall-panelling and particularly staircases, went through changes as well. Instead of the narrow spiral staircases which made things more difficult for attackers, handsome staircases were built, like the one in the picture.

The outstanding event of English architectural history in the period covered by this book was the building of St. Paul's Cathedral. The link with the Italian Renaissance is clearly seen in Wren's report on the defects of the old St. Paul's which was destroyed in the Great Fire of 1666. Wren suggested recasing the nave "after a good Roman Manner" instead of "the Gothick Rudeness of ye Old Design". His main suggestion was a dome. In spite of many difficulties the building was declared complete by Parliament in 1711, when Wren was seventy-nine. The dome of St. Paul's was the first to be built in

Cross-section of the dome of St. Paul's Cathedral, London

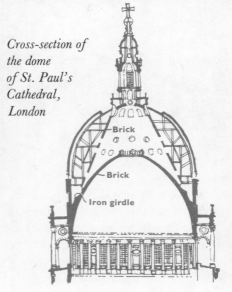

Brick

Brick

Iron girdle

England. It was a double dome invented by Wren so that it would be pleasing in appearance from the inside and the outside. If the dome was hemispherical (like half an orange), it would not look impressive from outside, but it would look good from the inside. If the dome had a steeper curve, it would look better from the outside, but would look like a funnel from the inside. Wren solved the problem by building a brick inner dome as shown in the diagram.

TOWN PLANNING

Italy. During the years 1481 to 1499 Leonardo da Vinci lived in Milan, and apart from carrying out works of military engineering he wrote about town planning. His ideas were, and still are, striking. He advised the ruler of Milan about the rebuilding of the city so as to avoid a repetition of the bad plagues of the years 1484–5. He suggested enlarging the city, saying:

". . . you will separate the great congregation of people who herd together like goats one on top of another, filling every place with foul odour and sowing seeds of pestilence and death."

Traffic was to run on two levels, the high-level street for pedestrians, the lower street for vehicles. Canals were to be used in some parts of the city instead of the low-level street. As a result goods could have been delivered from the canal side to the basements of houses. On the other hand visitors could have entered from the high-level street.

Italian cities often had their Renaissance developments blended with the existing pattern of building. In Turin the chessboard pattern of the old Roman fortified city was continued in the seventeenth-century extensions. Rome itself

▲ *St. Vedast's Church, London*

▲ *St. James, Garlickhythe, London*

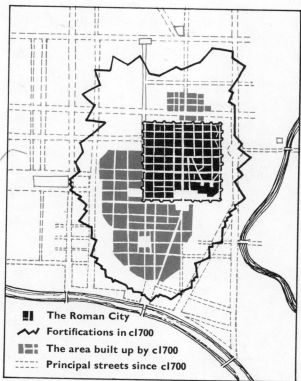

▮▮ The Roman City
〰 Fortifications in c1700
▮▮▮ The area built up by c1700
---- Principal streets since c1700

Plan of the city of Turin

had declined in population from a city of between 1¼ and 1½ millions in the second century A.D. to one of only 17 000 in the early fourteenth century. Rome revived in the fifteenth and sixteenth centuries despite the sacking of the city by the French in 1527.

France. The French, like the Italians, built on the grand scale and constructed some towns or parts of towns with avenues radiating from the centre like spokes of a wheel. The planned town of Richelieu (Indre-et-Loire), was founded by the French statesman Cardinal Richelieu. Two thousand workmen were employed to build his house. The town was to be the background to his magnificent quarters, an indication of the power and wealth of the great noblemen of seventeenth-century France. The site for the town was marshy and the drainage plan provided for the channelling of the water into moats which would surround the house and town. John Evelyn, the English diarist, visited the town on the 14th September, 1644, and wrote:

"We took post for Richelieu, passing by l'Isle Bouchard, a village in the way. The next day we arrived, and went to see the Cardinal's Palace, near it. The town is built in a low, marshy ground, having a narrow river cut by hand, very even and straight, capable of bringing up a small vessel. It consists of only one considerable street; the houses on both sides built exactly uniform, after a modern hand-some design. It has a large goodly market house, and place, opposite to which is the church built of freestone, having two pyramids of stone which standing hollow from the towers. . . . This pretty town is handsomely walled about and moated, with a kind of slight fortification, two fair gates and drawbridges."

The capital, Paris, was improved by Henry V (1589–1610) not just to make it beautiful, but to cut down overcrowding, to improve sanitation, and lastly, to provide work. He ordered the widening and paving of streets and the laying out of areas such as the Place Dauphine. His ambitious scheme for the North of Paris was abandoned after his death.

England. Even London was regarded, and rightly so in the poorer quarters, as a dangerous unhealthy place. A few years before the Great Plague of 1665 a mother wrote to her son, saying it was "so sikely a place", that he had better lead a well-ordered life or trouble would befall him. Her advice was accompanied by a present of a pair of riding stockings, a box of pies, cheeses and "biskates" to comfort his stomach.

The Great Fire of London in 1666, like the bombing of London during the Second World War, 1939–45, created a wonderful opportunity to plan and to carry out the rebuilding of the capital. Unfortunately in

London before the Great Fire

neither case did the city take anything like full advantage of the opportunity. In spite of this, by the eighteenth century, London was one of the best built capital cities in the world. One of the finest features of London was its squares. These were built piecemeal over a long period, and not as part of a grand plan as sometimes happened on the continent. The houses in the squares were built as places for gracious and civilized living: homes where free citizens could live in some privacy yet still be in a community. To many writers on town planning, this period in the history of London is an outstanding one.

Italian influence can be seen in the work of Inigo Jones, who laid out the squares in Lincoln's Inn Fields and Covent Garden before the Great Fire. After the fire, schemes were submitted for the rebuilding of London, among them being plans prepared by John Evelyn and Christopher Wren. None of the schemes was carried out.

Wren's plan for rebuilding London

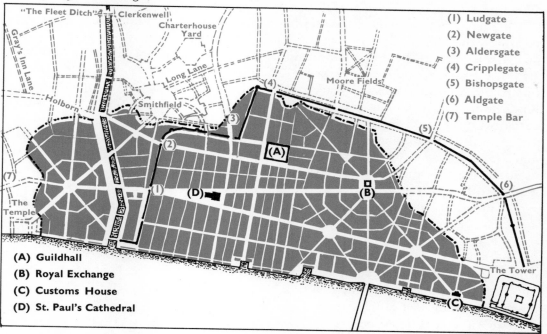

(1) Ludgate
(2) Newgate
(3) Aldersgate
(4) Cripplegate
(5) Bishopsgate
(6) Aldgate
(7) Temple Bar

(A) Guildhall
(B) Royal Exchange
(C) Customs House
(D) St. Paul's Cathedral

Clothing

Portrait of a Man, Titian   The National Gallery

COSTUME IN THE FIFTEENTH CENTURY

The Italian painters of the Renaissance portrayed the superb variety of dress for men and women at that time. Both sexes attached great importance to the perfection of their costume and their looks. As Burckhardt, an outstanding writer of this period wrote, "In no country of Europe since the fall of the Roman Empire was so much trouble taken to modify the face, the colour of the skin and the growth of the hair, as in Italy at this time."

This intense interest in personal appearance was also present in English people, particularly the wealthy classes. Not only did more people have money to spend on clothes, cosmetics and other means to improve appearances, but there was a much wider range of articles to be had than was the case in the Middle Ages. The stock of a fifteenth-century Leicester mercer included ready-made gowns of taffeta[1] or silk. In addition he had twenty different kinds of English and foreign cloth, "purses of gold cloth, belts, ribbons, skeins of Paris silk, children's stockings, silk coifs[2] and kerchiefs for nuns."

Changes took place in the country as well as in the town. Stuffed pillows replaced blocks of wood and instead of keeping their day clothes on when they went to bed, some country folk wore nightshirts.

Rivalry between the richer people in the expense and splendour of their dress grew in the fifteenth and sixteenth centuries. By the reign of Elizabeth, writers constantly drew attention to the craze for fashionable dress. The desire to be fashionable can be traced in changes that took place in the craft guilds in these two centuries. The uniform or livery worn by gildsmen in the Middle Ages was, like school uniform today, a sign of common interests and loyalties. During the fifteenth century gilds underwent many changes.

Typical of the changes were those experienced by the Gild of Pewterers. By the middle of the century some master craftsmen were much wealthier than the others. Changes in the rules of the gild were made so that the richer members could wear expensive livery, the colour of which might be changed from year to year. The poorer members, known as those "out of clothing", could not afford the livery and sat apart from those "in the clothing" at gild functions. By the middle of the sixteenth century clothing had become a way of showing differences between members of this gild. In England itself a similar change had taken place.

[1] Taffeta—a watered fabric of coarse plain woven silk.
[2] Coif—a close cap covering the top, back and sides of the head.

Man's dress

Bolstered and slashed sleeves

Woman's dress

The French farthingale

THE TUDORS

The meetings between French and English courtiers in the reign of Henry VIII led to the introduction of French fashions. Men's dress became rich and heavy as shown in the illustration. Fashions such as bolstered and slashed sleeves of the man's outer coat provoked this outburst from Petruchio in Shakespeare's *The Taming of the Shrew*:

"O mercy, God! what masquing stuff is
    here?
What's this? a sleeve? 'tis like a demi-
    cannon:
What, up and down, carved like an
    apple tart?
Here's a snip and nip and cut and slish
    and slash,
Like to a censer in a barber's shop!"

By the reign of Elizabeth there were two striking features of women's dress—the farthingale and the ruff. The farthingale was a skirt which was made to stand well away from the body by a framework of hoops. This gave the wearer remarkable width, but it does not seem to add much to the attraction of an Elizabethan lady.

The other feature, the ruff, was a type of pleated collar which was stiffened with wire and starch.

Frederick, Duke of Wurtemberg, visited London in 1592 and admired the dress of its inhabitants. He said, "The women have much more liberty than perhaps in any other place; they also know well how to make use of it, for they go dressed out in exceedingly fine clothes, and give all their attention to their ruffs and stuffs, to such a degree indeed, that, as I am informed, many a one does not hesitate to wear velvet in the streets, which is common with them, whilst at home they have not a piece of dry bread."

Ruffs

Clothing

Cavalier

Puritan

Cavalier

Puritan

Cavalier and Puritan dress

THE STUARTS

During the reign of James I, bombasted breeches and the farthingale were still worn, but dress became simpler in the reign of Charles I. The Puritans condemned extravagance in dress and in the illustrations you can see the difference between Cavalier and Puritan costume.

So far we have concentrated on an outline of the changes that took place in English dress; now we turn to France where the expense of the wardrobe and wig closet far outdid that of the kitchen.

An early seventeenth-century writer complained like his English counterpart of the effects of fashion. He said:

"Above all one must follow the fashion. I do not mean that set by one or two fops at court who, in order to cut a figure, now bury half their body in enormous boots, now plunge themselves up to the armpits into high breeches, now drown their faces in a hat with a brim as large as an Italian sunshade."

Louis XIII went bald early in life and as a result began to wear a wig. Courtiers followed his example and added further to the expense of keeping up with fashion. Wigs often weighed up to two pounds and cost from 2500 to 3000 francs. Wigs, false hair, powder and patches were the necessary equipment for the richer French women of that time. The patch, made of black silk or velvet, originated as a plaster to cover a pimple, but soon became part of a woman's make-up. Each patch had its own name according to its position on the face. One by the nose was a brazen; by the mouth a kisser; by the lower lip a discreet; in the middle of the cheek a gallant; and on the forehead a majestic. What with wigs, false hair, powder, patches and dresses it is clear that several hours would be taken up with the business of dressing.

Elaborate dress and rigid etiquette were

Brown double peaked
full bottomed wig
French 1690's

Patches and a wig

two of the features of life in the French court at Versailles. This is a description of how a well-brought-up Frenchman should behave at dinner:

"A man must wear his hat at dinner, but must refrain from putting it on until he has taken his place. The food to be passed round must be put on a clean plate; it is not, for instance, polite to extend a slice of mutton on the end of a fork or knife to the person for whom it is intended. Do not blow upon your food, do not throw what you cannot eat upon the floor, do not drink straight out of the soup tureen. To lick your knife or your fingers is the height of impropriety."

How different were the clothes and habits of the people of the French countryside, certainly the peasants and tradesmen and even some of the lesser noblemen and their families. The peasant wore a kind of overall, a short coat tied with cords, wide breeches, big gaiters generally made of leather, and hob-nailed shoes. Even if the peasant was rich the wife could not possibly keep up with the changes in fashion. She had to content herself with a dress that had to last a life-time. She made the attempt, however, to keep up with Paris with an ample skirt, a bodice stiffened with bones and flowered satin cuffs.

RESTORATION ENGLAND

The attempt to impose a Puritan life upon England during Cromwell's rule failed and was followed by a period of luxury. People wished to be extravagant again and there was a much wider range of goods from abroad. New goods from the East such as calicoes, chintzes, ginghams, cretonnes, and silks arrived and naturally people preferred these to the coarser home-made cloths. The manufacturers of woollen cloth were alarmed and asked the government for protection against imported Indian fabrics, which they described as:

"Tawdry, pie-spotted, flabby, ragged, low-priced, made by a parcel of heathens and pagans that worship the Devil and work for $\frac{1}{2}$d a day."

But the new fabrics came to stay and if you read about the Industrial Revolution in the cotton industry you will soon realise how the manufacturers and inventors spent their energies trying to produce cotton cloth fine enough to compete with fabrics from overseas.

In the remaining illustrations the chief changes in fashion can be followed through to the start of the eighteenth century.

Restoration costume

Clothing

Early 18th Century costume

Men's Wear. The doublet was lengthened until it eventually became a long skirted coat, the sleeves ending in wide cuffs. Waistcoats followed the same course, being lengthened and, unlike today, had long sleeves. Many buttons were used to adorn coats, whilst waistcoats were often elaborately embroidered. The wide pantaloons fastening at the knee became knee breeches and as you can see they were almost hidden by the long coats. Coloured silk stockings, shoes with buckles, a wig and a hat complete the picture of the man about town at this time.

Women's Dress. The outstanding feature of women's dress was the hoop which led to many difficulties for the wearer, as Joseph Gay described in *The Petticoat*:

"Yet found too late,
The petticoat too wide, the door too
strait;
Entrance by force she oft attempts to
gain,
Betty's assistance, too, she calls in vain,
The stubborn whalebone bears her
back again."

Industry and Trade

INTRODUCTION

The Spanish and Portuguese were pioneers in opening up the New World and the route to the East. Like most pioneers they were able to reap a good reward for their efforts. Philip II of Spain received between two and three million ducats every year from his overseas possessions. On hearing the news of the destruction of his armada off the coast of England in 1588, he could afford to say: "Great thanks do I render Almighty God, by whose generous hand I am gifted with such power, that I could easily, if I chose, place another fleet upon the sea."

The Spanish colonists shared in this wealth by managing the sugar estates of Cuba, or the gold and silver mines of Mexico and Peru. Surprisingly, however, the increase in trade which resulted from the development of the Spanish and Portuguese colonies was largely in the hands of foreigners, particularly the merchants of Antwerp.

The sixteenth century deserves to be called golden in Spanish history, because of its artistic and literary achievements. Despite this prosperity, little of Spain's wealth was devoted to the development of the homeland. Spain was considered a place of retirement, an old ancestral home where colonists went to rest and die. In contrast, countries such as England, the Dutch Republic and France used some of their increased wealth to develop their own resources and lay the basis of future industrial development.

The Dutch and World Trade

The basis of Dutch success in overseas and European trade was laid before the sixteenth century by the Dutch herring fleet which operated in the North Sea. This fleet consisted of large boats known as busses. They weighed about twenty or thirty tons and carried crews of between ten and fifteen men. They salted the fish on board and therefore did not have to return to port too often. The herring shoals were the Dutch "gold mine" and by 1620 about two thousand boats were at work in the North Sea.

Because the Dutch bought large quantities of timber from northern European states, such as Norway, they were able to obtain it at low prices. They used wind-driven sawmills and other labour-saving methods, in making their ships and the result was that Dutch ships became the cheapest in Europe. The Dutch controlled the carrying trade at sea because their rates were usually a half or a third less than other shippers.

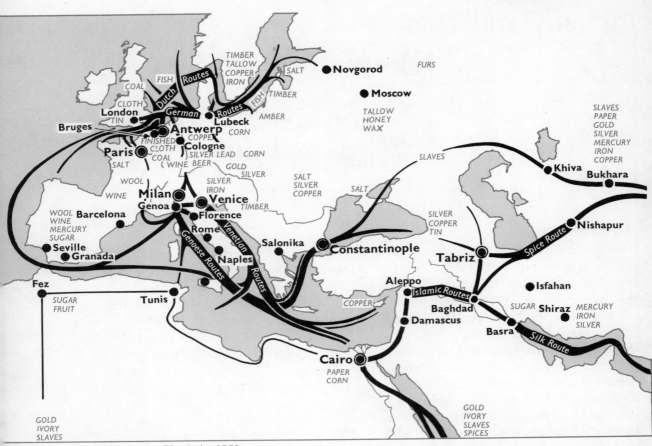

European Trade in 1550

The port of Antwerp was the centre for European and overseas trade, partly because of its ideal natural position as can be seen from the map and partly because of the services provided by the Dutch merchants and shippers. Antwerp kept its key position in trade until after the middle of the sixteenth century. From that time it began to decline, until its revival in the nineteenth century.

English Foreign Trade in the 16th and 17th Centuries

England was in an ideal position to take advantage of the discovery of the new routes to America and the East, but she did not take much part in these discoveries until after 1550. English industries needed more markets for their goods. This is why trading companies such as the Muscovy Company (founded in 1555), the Levant Company (1581) and the East India Company (1600) were set up. Before these companies were set up trade was largely in the hands of the Merchant Adventurers. This company dealt in manufactured goods, such as English woollen cloth, which was sold at their headquarters in Antwerp. Entrance to the company was by an eight year apprenticeship, or by a heavy entrance fee. Often the sons of nobles became members and, not unnaturally, the company had a great deal of political and social influence. These companies took the place of the merchant guilds which were described in Book 1. Trade had become a matter of national concern and in the reign of Elizabeth, English enterprise began to flourish.

Increased trade with the East and America brought many new articles into the lives of English people. Tea, coffee, sugar, tobacco, calico and muslin began by being luxuries, but in time became necessities. Apart from these goods there were two commodities which had a very important place in trade between America and Europe. These were precious metals such as silver, and slaves. England was late in the race for colonies in America and had to gain precious metals by trade, or by piracy. She was not so late in entering the slave trade.

It was in 1503 that the first negro slaves were shipped to America. In 1562 John Hawkins, a Plymouth merchant, entered the West Indian slave trade. This trade was not looked upon as wrong by Europeans, for it had existed for centuries in the Mediterranean, where the galleys of Christian and Moslem countries were rowed by slaves. Estimates of the number of slaves landed in America between 1600 and 1900 are as follows:

1600–1700	2 750 000
1700–1800	7 000 000
1800–1900	4 000 000

In the middle of the seventeenth century this trade was largely in the hands of the Dutch but by the end of the eighteenth century England had gained most of the trade.

The business of buying the slaves is vividly described in this passage from the journal of the captain of *The Hannibal* who sailed on the triangular trip from England to Africa, and then to the West Indies in 1693–94:

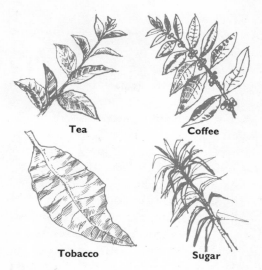

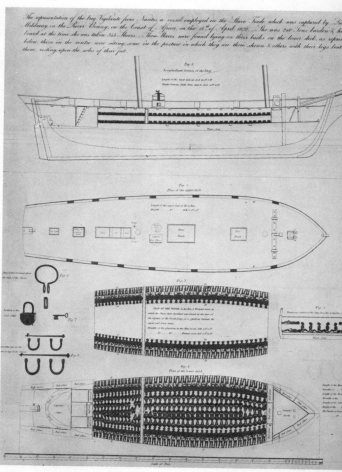

Plan of Stowage of Slaves on the Vigilante

127

Trade

"This morning I went ashore at Whidaw, accompany'd by my doctor and purser, Mr. Clay, the present Captain of the *East India Merchant*, his Doctor and purser, and about a dozen of our seamen for our guards arm'd, in order here to reside till we could purchase 1300 negro slaves, which was the number we both wanted to compleat 700 for *The Hannibal* and 650 for *The East India Merchant*. . . .

"As soon as the king understood of our landing, he sent two of his cappashiers or noblemen to compliment us at our factory. . . . According to promise we attended his majesty with samples of our goods, and made our agreement about the prices, though not without some difficulty . . . the King's slaves, if he had any, were the first offered for sale . . . then the cappashiers each brought out his slaves according to his degree and quality, the greatest first and our surgeon examined them well in all kinds, to see that they were sound in wind and limb, making them jump, stretch out their arms swiftly, looking in their mouths to judge of their age. . . .

"When our slaves were come to the seaside, our canoes were ready to carry them off to the longboat, if the sea permitted, and she conveyed them aboard ship, where the men were all put in irons, two and two shackled together to prevent their mutiny or swimming ashore."

Some slaves preferred, if they could break free, to leap into the sea and drown rather than suffer the dreadful voyage and endless labour in the West Indies. Three hundred and twenty of the negroes taken aboard the *Hannibal* died between 25th August and 4th November when the ship reached the Barbados. The survivors were sold either directly to the planters or to dealers who took them from plantation to plantation until they were all sold. One can feel only anger and shame when the lot of the African in the West Indies is compared to the life led by the planters or the families who lived in luxury on the income gained from property in those islands.

English sailors and merchants were interested in trading with the people of Muscovy, or Russia, as well. In 1553 Sir Hugh Willoughby with Richard Chancellor, Pilot Major, "the first discoverer by sea of the kingdom of Moscovia", sailed for the White Sea. Only one ship, that commanded by Chancellor, survived. He met the Tsar, Ivan the Terrible, and soon trade between England and Russia began. The ships sent to Russia by the Muscovy company in 1557 took various types of cloth and nine barrels of pewter, received in return wax, flax, tallow and train (whale) oil. Other goods such as furs, walrus ivory, hemp, salt fish and corn were available.

The East India Company was founded in 1600 and had full control—a monopoly—of all trade with Asia. It founded trading depots, or factories, in India at Surat, Madras, Calcutta and Bombay. From these depots the Company gradually built up its control of much of India. In 1674 a surgeon, Dr. Fryer, visited Surat and described the factory. It was built of stone and timber with the warehouse on the ground floor. Above were the rooms where the company employees lived. When ships arrived native traders came to the factory. Trading hours were from 10 to 12 in the morning and from 4 p.m. until nightfall. The Company's employees were very badly paid, even the president at Surat received only £300 a year in 1674. As a result, many of the employees of the company traded on their own account and some of them made fortunes.

INDUSTRY

It was during the sixteenth and seventeenth centuries that Europe, particularly the north, began to go through changes in industry that were followed by the Industrial Revolution. Great Britain is one of the best examples of industrial change in Northern Europe. She had a good supply of coal and iron, the basic materials for industrialisation. Furthermore, her manufacturers were quick to increase the size of their works and to introduce machinery and the latest methods. These changes made the finished goods cheaper, and therefore they became more in demand.

The Coal Industry

As you can see from the diagram, coal had many uses and was wanted in ever increasing quantities. The result was that deeper shafts had to be sunk to obtain the coal. As the deeper seams of coal were mined, flooding became a major problem. No amount of ingenuity in the use of the old forms of power could solve this problem. The answer came with the discovery of steam power. (See section on power.)

The uses of coal

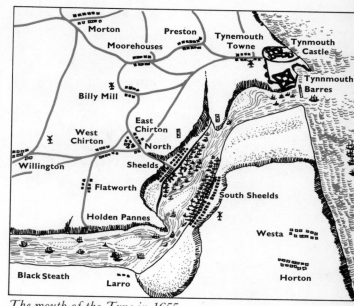

The mouth of the Tyne in 1655

The most important coalfield in England in the sixteenth and seventeenth centuries was the one in Durham and Northumberland. Let us try to reconstruct what it must have been like if you had arrived at the mouth of the Tyne in one of the ships which regularly carried coal from that river to the Thames and London. The ship's ballast was discharged and coal was taken on from the keels

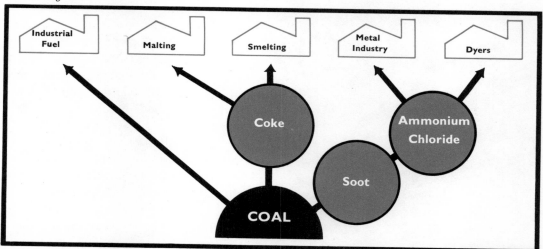

which had come to South Shields, at the mouth of the river. The keelmen, like the miners, were often looked down on at this time. A customs officer, given the job of pressing keelmen into service decided against it because the presence of "such nasty creatures on board would do more harm than good". The coal was loaded on to the keels from the staithes at the side of the river. In some cases it had arrived at the staithes in wagons drawn by horses along wooden railways.

A surprise awaited the stranger who went to a pit in the early seventeenth century, for near to the pithead would be heaps of coal, one for each partner in the colliery. If some partners had bigger shares than others the overman at the pit made sure that more coal went on their heaps. Each partner arranged the sale of his own coal. Many collieries employed over 100 miners, and in the pits of the North-East no women worked below ground. The hewers cut the coal, the barrowmen pushed the trams to the shaft bottom, and boys did many of the other jobs in the mine.

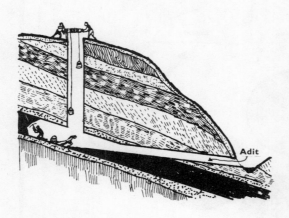

An early coal mine

The Iron Industry

When you read that between 12 000 and 18 000 cannon balls were fired into Magdeburg during each day of a siege in 1631, you realise that the demands of war on the iron industry were considerable. Iron was also used for many things in peacetime—firedogs, pots, pans and boilers. Unfortunately for the iron masters there was a timber shortage and consequently a charcoal shortage in England during the sixteenth, seventeenth and eighteenth centuries. Areas such as the Weald were deforested and the price of wood rose.

The pig iron which came from the blast furnace was beaten into wrought iron at the forge. Furnace and forge used charcoal as a fuel, so both had to be situated near to forests. The wood shortage led to the need for an alternative fuel. The discovery of coke solved this problem.

The Woollen Industry

At an earlier date this industry had been situated in the towns, but by the sixteenth century many craftsmen were moving to the country districts. In the country they were free from the regulations of the gilds. It would be easy to build up a picture of the contented weaver and his family in their own cottage busily employed making cloth, and growing much of their own food. This picture would leave out the clothier who took the wool to the weavers and collected the finished cloth. Without the clothier many weavers might have found it difficult to obtain a regular supply of wool and a market for their cloth, so the clothier was in a powerful position.

The Halifax Act of 1555 safeguarded the position of the small producers of cloth and gave a vivid description of these men, only able to buy small quantities of wool, unable to afford a horse to carry it and compelled to "carrye the same to their houses, some three, four and five myles of, upon their Headdes and Backes".

After the wool was brought home, it was first spread out on hurdles, where it was beaten, and any foreign matter was picked out. Oil, or sometimes butter, was mixed with the wool and when this was finished it was ready for carding. The next operation was to spin the wool. The illustrations show you some of the operations that followed, until finally the cloth was fit to go to the local market and then probably on to London and the continent.

Some men owned factories where many craftsmen were employed. One such establishment, owned by John Winchcombe of Newbury, was described in a ballad by Thomas Deloney:

"Within one room being large and long
  There stood two hundred looms full
    strong:

Two hundred men the truth is so
Wrought in these looms all in a row . . .
And in another place hard by,
An hundred women merrily
Were carding hard with joyful cheer
Who singing sate with voices clear.
And in a chamber close beside,
Two hundred maidens did abide
In petticoats of Stammel red
And milk white kerchiefs on their
    head, . . .
And spinning so with voices meet
Like nightingales they sing full sweet.
Then to another roome came they
Where children were in poore array:
And every one sat picking wool,
The finest from the coarse to cull."

Hand-cards of the eighteenth century

A distaff of the early seventeenth century

A spinning wheel

The winder

A weaver at a hand-loom

Similar large factories were set up in other parts of England so, as in the coal industry, the size of establishments was beginning to increase and to foreshadow the Industrial Revolution.

Power

The tower mill

POWER

Steam power was developed only towards the end of the seventeenth century. We must deal here, therefore, with the developments in the use of the old sources of power, such as the tower mill, and the background to the introduction of the steam engine in the eighteenth century.

The Tower Mill. It is often worth thinking of the typical miller as a crafty man who believed in letting his mill do as much of the heavy work as possible. The tower mill with its fantail could be left to keep itself in the wind, for as the wind changed direction, it rotated the vanes of the fantail and kept the main sails in the wind. These mills were built of timber or brick; if brick, they were tarred over to prevent the wet from getting into the brickwork. Improvements in iron manufacture led to a greater use of iron for gears and winches.

Power and Mines. The growth of coal mining in the sixteenth and seventeenth centuries led to deeper and deeper pits being sunk. As pits increased in depth the problem of drainage became acute. In mines on the continent all sorts of devices were invented to raise water, many appearing in the pages of Agricola's work *De re metallica.* Some of these methods

were copied in England, but they were often cumbersome and expensive. Newcomen's "fire machine" in 1712 provided a better means of draining mines.

A rag and chain pump

Guericke's Experiment c. 1654

The Early Steam Engine. The scientists of the Renaissance studied air pressure. Galileo started such a study, which was finished by his pupil Torricelli. The result of their study was the discovery that air pressure at sea level supported a vertical column of mercury 76 centimetres in height and that pressure fell with increasing height above sea level. Scientists wanted to use this pressure so they made devices which created a vacuum beneath a piston. Air pressure would then work the piston. The illustration shows the experiment carried out by Otto von Guericke to prove the power of air pressure. Sixteen powerful horses were unable to pull the evacuated sphere apart.

Thomas Savery invented a practical steam pump, and by 1702 had this advertisement published:

"Captain Savery's engines which raise water by the force of Fire in any reasonable quantities and to any height, being now brought to perfection and ready for publick use; These are to give notice to all proprietors of Mines and Collieries which are incumbered with Water, that they may be furnished with Engines to drain the same, at his Workshouse in Salisbury Court, London, against the Old Playhouse, where it may be seen working on Wednesdays and Saturdays in every week from 3 to 6 in the afternoons. . . ."

Thomas Newcomen's engine was a great improvement, but we must leave the story of its development to Book 3.

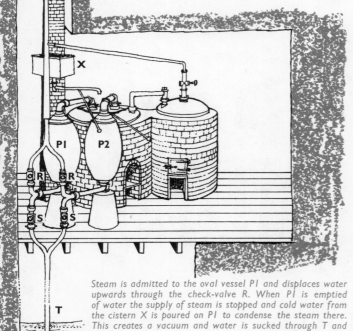

Steam is admitted to the oval vessel P1 and displaces water upwards through the check-valve R. When P1 is emptied of water the supply of steam is stopped and cold water from the cistern X is poured on P1 to condense the steam there. This creates a vacuum and water is sucked through T and valve S. P2 is filled with steam while P1 is being cooled.

Captain Savery's Miner's Friend

Transport

Elizabethan coach

TRANSPORT BY LAND

The improvement of roads was closely connected with the development of trade and government policy, and it was in the eighteenth century that the really important changes took place. In England the Industrial Revolution led to a desperate need for better roads. In France the national policy of road making and training road engineers set an example to the rest of Europe. These changes are dealt with in the next volume. The story of transport in this section is one of bad roads, good ideas not put into practice, and the beginnings of improvement.

In the year 1598 the Great North Road near to the town of Ware was described as:

"very ruinous, and washed away by the inflood of water thereupon, so that for a long time it hath been impassable for men as well as horses".

This was not the only English main road in a bad state, for roads generally were bad. There was little money spent on new roads in Europe in the fifteenth and sixteenth centuries, and, just as important, there was little interest in scientific methods of road building. In many places bundles of faggots together with stones were used for filling pot-holes, in the belief that the mixture improved drainage.

The men of the Renaissance studied the writings of the Greeks and Romans of the Ancient World, which included their techniques of road building. They rediscovered scientific road building, but unfortunately these ideas did not often get put into practice. Andreas Palladio (1518–80) and Vincenzo Scamozzi (1552–1616) outlined better ways of road building. Scamozzi thought roads in country areas should be well drained, wide, straight and made of lasting materials; ideas which English road engineers such as McAdam put into practice at a later date.

Strong kings such as Henry VIII of England and Henry IV of France made important changes, showing how central direction was needed before improvements took place. Henry VIII appointed a "Master of the Posts" (post comes from the Latin "positus"—a man placed at a given point) who arranged for men at post-houses to keep horses ready for the king's messengers. About 1580, in the reign of Elizabeth, the regular routes were London to Dover, London to Berwick, London to Holyhead, London to Paris through Rouen, and to Bruges through Antwerp. Along these routes the post went once a week.

Transport

Henry IV of France started the office of Grand Voyer de France; this involved the direction of all road building and repairs in France. The Government helped provinces to build roads by loans which were repaid from the salt tax.

Perhaps you will get a better idea of the state of inland transport if we take a more detailed look at England at the start of the seventeenth century.

There were only three ways of carrying goods or passengers from one place to another—by sea along the coast, by river or by road. The most important river

Ports and navigable rivers from Camden's seventeenth-century map

routes were the Thames, the Severn, the Trent and the Great Ouse. A town such as London needed many goods from other parts of England and the continent, and the Thames was the great highway for such traffic. The laden barges brought cheeses and corn from Oxford, bales of cloth from Reading and the west, timber from the forests of Berkshire and on their return journey they would take "sea coles" which had come from Newcastle and luxuries such as spices, sugar and tobacco.

It was very much cheaper to carry goods by river or round the coast, so roads were often used only where other means of transport were not available. Most roads were for local use and the illustrations from Bewick's *History of Quadrupeds* give you some idea of the hazards of road transport.

Before 1675 there were no clear maps of the main highways of England, but in that year John Ogilby, mapmaker to Charles II, published a book of the chief roads of England and Wales. Ogilby employed a man to measure distances with a cyclometer while he recorded the direction of the roads. His book became famous and small editions were produced which could fit into a traveller's pocket.

The commonest sight on the roads in the good travelling months of spring and summer were the strings of packhorses. Each beast would carry either panniers, crates or bales which weighed up to half a ton. These packhorse trains kept to fixed routes and times, and were really the goods trains of the seventeenth century.

Wheeled traffic increased in the sixteenth and seventeenth centuries and attempts were made to construct better vehicles. Coaches were introduced into England in the mid-sixteenth century, and they take their name from Kotze in Hungary where they were first made. The people in the coach found it uncomfortable for the coach had no springs, and had only curtains to protect them from the weather.

Coach building improved a great deal in the reign of Charles II, especially after the founding of the Company of Coach and Coach-Harness Makers in 1677. In many respects the framework of coaches of this time resembled the German waggon.

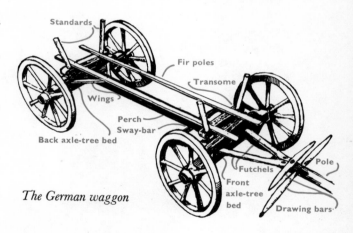

The German waggon

The front wheels and axle were not rigidly attached to the body as were those on a sixteenth-century coach; they were pivoted, so the coach was much easier to handle round a corner. The body of the coach was suspended from the standards by leather straps; this was the first attempt at springing. Mr. Pepys records

Pack horses

A Coach and Four

the trials of a coach buyer in his diary for November 1668. He visited the coach-makers in Cow Lane, London, and:

"did see several, and at last did pitch upon a little chariott, whose body was framed, but not covered . . . and we are mightily pleased with it, it being light, and will be very genteel and sober . . .".

The proud owner regularly recorded the outings he made in his coach after it was complete, just as a present-day motorist will tell of the virtues of his latest purchase.

the town coach. Strength was the important consideration on bad roads and until roads improved the lighter types of coach could not be used for travelling long distances.

In the English midlands the four-wheeled waggon replaced the two-wheeled waggon on many of the bigger farms during the seventeenth and eighteenth centuries. These were used at harvest time in particular. Illustrations of the two main types, the box waggon and the bow waggon can be seen in Book 3.

A stage waggon with passengers

The waggons used for long distance travel had to be much stronger, and they look heavy and clumsy compared with

The first Turnpike Act was passed in 1663, but it was not until the period 1730–1750 that turnpikes were set up in large numbers.

Carrier with a two-wheeled cart

TRANSPORT BY SEA

We admire men who take risks to make great discoveries, and the fifteenth and sixteenth centuries provide us with many examples of such men, especially the sailors who discovered the New World, and many new sea routes. Behind their successes lay changes in ship construction and navigation; changes which, along with their courage and skill, made these discoveries possible.

The development of the ships in the sixteenth and seventeenth centuries

The typical ships of the Mediterranean at the start of the sixteenth century were the war galley and the trading galley. A galley was normally about 40 metres long and five metres amidships. There were twenty-five to thirty benches on each side of the galley and three oarsmen sat on

A Mediterranean galley

each bench. These galleys were still used by some Mediterranean countries up to the eighteenth century. The lot of the galley slaves is summed up as follows:

"If there is a hell on earth it is in the galleys where rest is unknown."

These galleys generally made for harbour at night if it was possible, and in calm or head winds they had to anchor or remain rolling about at sea. Moreover the

galley was expensive to run for it had a large crew. These facts should help you to understand why these ships were replaced by the full-rigged ship.

A three-masted merchantman

One of the earliest illustrations of the three-masted carrack is on the Seal of Louis de Bourbon, dated 1466. The ship has a large mainmast, a foremast and a mizzen mast which had a lateen sail. The ship looks strong rather than fast, and most important, it could make use of almost any wind because of its combination of sails. The rudder, too, was fully developed, the tiller passing into the hull of the ship. This new ship was fit for a voyage of discovery for it was easier to handle, much stronger than previous ships and could carry stores and people in its hull. The credit for perfecting these new ships must go to the shipwrights of Spain, Portugal and Brittany.

The full-rigged ships made long, dangerous voyages possible, but, strangely, the ships used by Columbus and Magellan were not of good quality. Columbus's

The evolution of the sail plan, 1430-1600

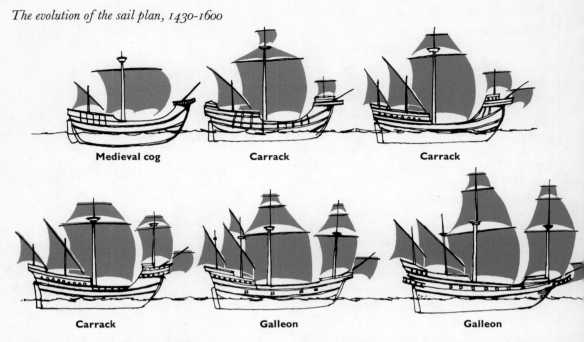

Medieval cog   Carrack   Carrack

Carrack   Galleon   Galleon

ships were chosen and manned with little care, and one writer said of Magellan's vessels, bought at Cadiz, that:

"They are very old and patched, and I should be sorry to sail even for the Canaries in them, for their ribs are as soft as butter."

These facts underline the courage and skill of the sailors of the Renaissance.

Henry VIII's Navy. Henry's navy was typical of European shipping in the early sixteenth century. His greatest ship, the *Henry Grace à Dieu* weighed 1000 tons, carried twenty-one heavy brass guns, 130 iron guns and had a crew of 700 men. A list of ships of the Royal Navy of 1546 divided them into four classes: ships, galleasses, pinnaces and barges. The ships had high castles, unlike the galleasses which had lower castles and beakheads like the Mediterranean galleys. The pinnaces were small ships and the barges smaller still, only twenty tons each and fitted with oars.

The galleon was an improved fighting ship developed by the Portuguese and by the time the Spanish Armada sailed in 1588 both English and Spanish navies were equipped with these ships.

Construction of ships

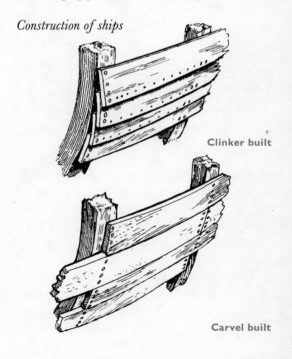

Clinker built

Carvel built

Ship Construction and Guns

The improvement of ships and guns went hand in hand during Henry VIII's reign. Instead of ships being clinker built they were carvel built as shown in the diagram. The hulls of ships were more strongly built and provision was made to carry the guns broadside. Ships had square sterns which had two portholes through which poked the stern chase guns. The hulls were covered with a mixture of oil, turpentine and resin. Later, in Elizabeth's reign, the *Ark Royal*'s hull was sheathed to shield it from attack by the ship-worm. Elm boards about one centimetre thick were nailed over layers of Stockholm tar and hair, sufficient to deter the most ambitious ship-worm.

A great deal of wood was needed to make a ship: a large warship required some 2000 oak trees. These trees take a hundred years to reach maturity, and could not be grown on less than 20 hectares of woodland. We know quite a lot about the design of warships of the seventeenth century because shipwrights often made models before they built ships. Many of these models have survived and can be seen in museums.

Phineas Pett was a Woolwich shipwright in the reign of Charles I and built amongst other ships the *Sovereign of the Seas*. The timber for the ship came from Chopwell woods near Newcastle. His sawyers took moulds with them to the oaks in these woods and nailed them to likely trees. These moulds were full-sized patterns of various shapes needed for the construction of the hull, and if the natural twists and curves of the tree matched the mould it would be cut down. In all 2500 trees were chosen, felled and sawn up. They were loaded on to waggons and sent to Newcastle and Sunderland and then they went by ship to London. The

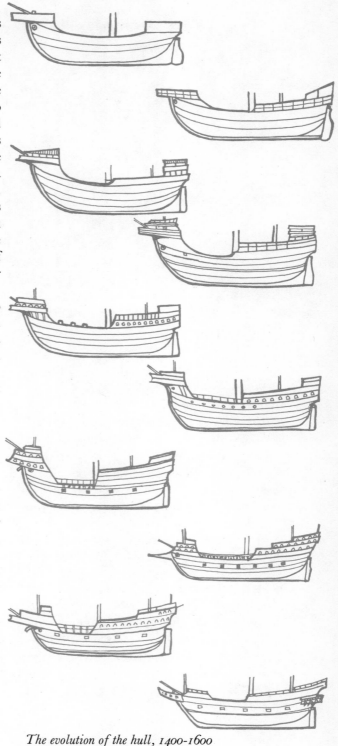

The evolution of the hull, 1400-1600

141

The Ark Royal, 1588

Sovereign of the Seas took about three years to build and when finished was a beautiful ship with plenty of gilded decoration, a typical feature of Stuart ships.

Guns. Cumbersome breech loaders lashed on to baulks of timber had been used on fourteenth-century ships. They were put in the castles: places ill-fitted for guns. The best place for them was as near to the waterline as possible, so that the roll of the ship would be cut down to a minimum and give the gunners the best chance of hitting their targets. To cut holes near the waterline for gun ports seemed dangerous and the *Mary Rose*, an English warship, heeled over in a strong wind in 1545 and water rushed in through the gun ports and sank her in a few minutes. These difficulties were overcome and Sir Walter Raleigh compared the faster ships designed by Sir John Hawkins to the Spanish galleons in these words:

"The greatest ships are the least service-able, (they) go very deep in water, and of marvellous expense . . . less nimble, less manageable, and seldom employed. A ship of 600 tons will carry as good guns as one of 1200 tons, and will turn her broadsides twice before the greater can turn once."

At this time the demi-cannon threw a ball of thirty-two pounds whilst the smallest gun used in the Elizabethan navy, a minion, threw a ball of three pounds. Larger cannon than the "demi" or half cannon were used in other European navies.

A ship's cannon

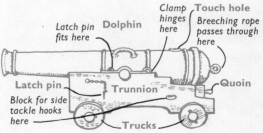

NAVIGATION

The astrolabe

The sailors of the fifteenth century had only a few simple instruments and poor maps to help them find their way. Their compass-needle was mounted on a "card" and the lubber line was marked on the deck of the ship. They found which latitude they were in by the use of the astrolabe and astronomer's tables. The astrolabe was used to find the height in degrees of the sun on a particular day, then, with this information—the date and the height of the sun—the navigator could read off the latitude in the tables.

The Pole Star could be used at night, and observation of this star led Columbus to note the deviation of his compass. It pointed to the magnetic and not the true north, a fact sailors still have to take into account when navigating. Later the cross staff was used to measure the height of the sun. The glare of the sun could be extremely uncomfortable when a cross staff

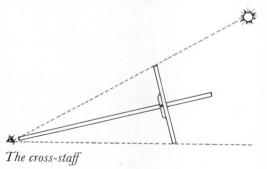

The cross-staff

was used, and by the seventeenth century the back staff was in use. With this instrument the observer turned his back on the sun. Sailors had no means of knowing their longitude, so what they did was to sail to a latitude in the general direction of their destination then sail along that line.

Near to the coast a sailor of Western Europe would use tide-diagrams. The English called these sailing directions rutters, the French routiers, and the information recorded on them included rocks, shoals, tides and landmarks. Near to shore the sailors could take soundings with lead and line, the lead being greased so that it picked up a sample of the sea bottom.

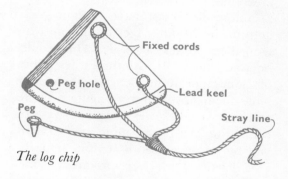

The log chip

The speed of a ship was difficult to calculate until the practice of using a log chip came into use in the seventeenth century. A log chip attached to a line marked with knots was thrown into the sea. As the ship progressed the log line was played out until some sand in a glass, which had begun to run when the log chip had settled, had completed its twenty-eight second drop into the lower part of the container. The length of cord between the knots was forty-seven and one-third feet, the time twenty-eight seconds, and by counting the number of knots it would be quite simple to work out the speed of the ship in sea miles per hour, knots.

The Art of War

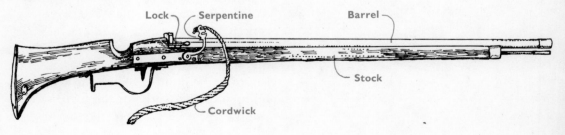

An arquebus

1. ON LAND

The use of gunpowder and firearms in the early fourteenth century was one of the greatest changes in the waging of war. It made war more difficult to organise and much more expensive.

Gunpowder must have been a great help in the Middle Ages to anyone who wished to attack a castle. One could bombard the walls with the earliest types of cannon or mine beneath them and blow them up. Military engineers were soon employed, however, to find ways of combating the use of mine and cannon and by the seventeenth century remarkable defence works were produced. Vauban was one of the outstanding engineers and worked in France and the Netherlands.

Weapons

Firearms. During the sixteenth and seventeenth centuries a number of differ-

ent hand firearms were made. Amongst them were the matchlock and the flintlock. There were three main parts to these guns: the barrel which contained the explosive charge and directed the shot; the lock which fired the charge; and the stock which helped the holder of the gun to grasp it firmly and to aim it in comfort.

The loading and the firing of these weapons took a long time, as a detailed description of these operations confirms. With the barrel pointing upwards a charge of gunpowder was put down it and kept in place by a wad of paper which was rammed down tightly. A lead ball was then put down the barrel and a second

A matchlock musket

Lock — Serpentine   Barrel

Stock

Cordwick

144

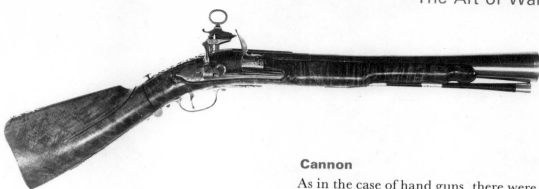

A flintlock blunderbuss

wad of paper rammed down to keep it in place. If this was not done the ball might roll out of the barrel before the gun was fired. These guns were heavy, so a rest was used while the priming pan was filled with a small amount of fine gunpowder. This pan was next to the touchhole so that when the man set fire to the priming, the charge in the barrel was set off. The priming was set off by a slow match. This was made of twine, and soaked in saltpetre so that once lit it kept glowing. Soldiers would often smoke their pipes during a battle, not just to settle their nerves, but to light their matches when they were needed. The loading, and especially the firing, of a matchlock in wet weather were very difficult. The development of the flintlock did much to overcome this, for if the gun misfired the first time the lock could be cocked and fired again.

The illustration of the flintlock shows the flint held in a screw-clamp. This was cocked by pulling it back against a spring. The trigger released the arm and the flint struck a rough plate above the firing pan so that the priming was set alight by sparks.

Even some of the best firearms used by armies in the seventeenth and eighteenth centuries had a range not much greater than a cross-bow.

Cannon

As in the case of hand guns, there were many types of early cannon, but by the end of the seventeenth century they were simply known by the weight of the ball they fired. There were twenty-four, sixteen, twelve, eight and four pounders listed among French cannon for 1697. A mould had to be made for each cannon in the sixteenth century. As the guns were cast straight from the smelting furnace the metal was impure, and by the time the gunner received the finished product he had to study it very carefully for its individual qualities. It might fire a little to

A knight in armour firing a cannon

A Cannon foundry in the sixteenth century

the left of where the gunner aimed it, or its range might be shorter than other guns of the same type. The illustration shows you a sixteenth century bronze cannon foundry; note the scene in the top right hand corner—a good advertisement for their products!

Apart from the cannon there was the mortar which had a short, wide bore and fired an explosive bomb. As the bomb had to be lit before firing the mortar, the bombardier ran the risk of the bomb exploding inside the mortar. This risk was overcome in the seventeenth century by being able to light the fuse of the bomb through the touch hole. Hand-grenades, small-fused bombs thrown by hand, were developed and the first companies of grenadiers, or throwers of grenades, were raised about 1670.

Fortifications

Look at the two photographs opposite of types of fortification and note as many of the differences between the two as you can. Fortifications grew in size and complexity as you can see in the second photograph. A position of natural strength was as important for siting a fortification in the sixteenth and seventeenth centuries as it had been in the Middle Ages. For example a medieval castle at Corfe was defended in the English Civil War with some success. On the other hand, you could not rely on stout high walls, a broad moat and a good supply of food to withstand a siege once cannon, mortar and mining techniques were known to your enemies. Your defence had to be active, and your fortifications had to give you the best chance to use your firearms to kill your enemies without giving them an opportunity to kill you.

As armies were larger and better organised a defence work might have to contain a few thousand men, much artillery and plenty of supplies. It would need good and well-defended supply lines and might well be situated on, or near to, a river or major road. Many important defence works were centred on towns and were ringed with trenches and parapets cunningly placed to give the very best positions to the defenders.

If the attackers managed to drive you from the defence works, shown as an inset in the diagram, it would be of little use to them, for they would be open to fire from the main defence works behind. The lay-out of the main defence works had to be planned so that the greatest amount of cross-fire was possible. This was done by constructing bastions.

The great French engineer Vauban planned his defences in depth. As Voltaire wrote of Vauban's defence works in his *Age of Louis XIV*, "He constructed them according to a new method of his, which is today accepted by all expert engineers. Astonishment was expressed at seeing the towns surrounded by outworks hardly higher than the surrounding country. High and towering fortifications were only the more exposed to the battering of artillery; the lower they were made the

Richmond Castle Keep, Yorkshire

less liable they were to attack." In the course of his work he had to study soils, to survey, to plan excavations of large ditches and to construct ramps. This involved him in work which was similar to that carried out in peaceful occupations such as canal and railway building at a later date. So many of the skills used for making war could be turned to peaceful use when the opportunity arose; Vauban for instance gave advice on the construction of the Canal du Midi in 1686.

Namur, a fortified town in Eastern France

Inset: Fortified Town—Vauban's method of fortification

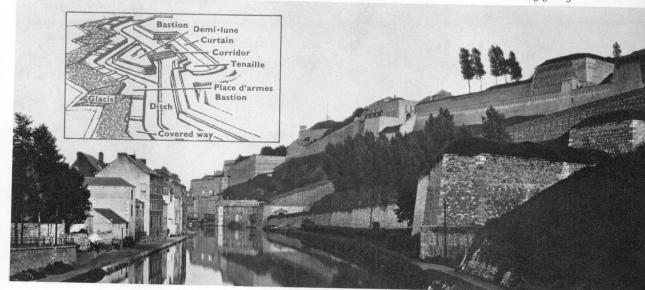

The Art of War

THE ARMIES OF EUROPE

War-making could be a profitable profession in the sixteenth and seventeenth centuries, and many mercenaries were employed by European monarchs. The word "mercenary" means "working merely for a reward" and such a person would sell his services to the highest bidder. Moreover, mercenaries would move quite freely from one army to another as one contract ended and another began. You may think that this was a strange state of affairs, for you probably think men went to war more from a sense of duty than for money.

Mercenaries became less important when permanent armies were raised in Europe. Perhaps the first example of a standing army was the one raised by the Spaniards to fight in the Netherlands in the sixteenth century. Later other European countries raised standing armies and with them came the common features of a present-day soldier's life—officers, uniform, inspections and discipline.

In France and Prussia, officers were usually men of noble descent or great wealth. Commissions were sold by officers. When an officer left his regiment he sold his commission and the buyer in some cases would not be a trained soldier. This system continued in the English army until 1871! A strict disciplinarian is often called a "martinet". This was the name of the first Inspector-General of the French army, who made it efficient.

Infantry

The English longbowmen and the Swiss pikemen proved their worth against heavily armoured knights before firearms came into general use. Early firearms took so long to reload that the soldiers who

A musketeer

A pikeman

fired them had to be defended by pikemen, otherwise they would have been cut down by cavalry charges. Henry IV of France (1589–1610) had only two weapons for his infantry, the pike and the matchlock. They were well-disciplined and grouped into regiments. Part of the training consisted of mock battles which took place in winter quarters.

At the time of the English Civil War, 1642–46, the infantry of the two sides was divided into pikemen and musketeers. The pike was about six metres long and required skilful handling. With the butt end of the pike firmly against his back foot the pikeman could stand in a position of lunge, the pike pointing towards his enemy. A line of pikemen could form a bristling wall against a charge and in some ways were similar to the Macedonian phalanx mentioned in Book 1.

The Renaissance studies of the Ancient World led to renewed interest in Roman military methods. In the Low Countries these studies led to the training of soldiers in digging, which had a good effect on discipline. William Louis of Friesland paid attention to the scientific discoveries of the Renaissance and was probably the first general to use a church tower as an observation point for his telescope. Other changes he brought in were the time-fuse for hand-grenades, and the curb-bit for cavalry.

Cavalry

European cavalry were usually armed with pistols and tactics did not change until the time of the Swedish king Gustavus Adolphus (1611–32). The tactic commonly used by lines of cavalry was called "the caracole". It consisted of a line of cavalry halting, firing at the enemy, then wheeling off to the rear to wait for their next turn. Gustavus Adolphus ordered his men to charge without halting and to fire only at the last minute. Such a charge could have a terrifying effect on the enemy.

Prince Rupert, the Cavalier commander, taught his cavalry to use these shock tactics during the English Civil War. At two or three o'clock in the afternoon of 23rd October, 1642, Rupert's cavalry used a Swedish charge to drive the left wing of Parliament's army off the battlefield at Edgehill. If there was a victory in this battle it was Rupert's, and it was his cavalry that gained it. His opponents, especially Cromwell, knew they could only turn from defence to attack when they had cavalry of similar quality.

A Cromwellian cavalryman

Cromwell copied and improved upon Rupert's methods, and his Ironsides played a major part in the victory at Marston Moor in July 1644. In a letter to his brother after the battle, Cromwell wrote:

"The left wing, which I commanded, being our own horse, saving a few Scots in our rear, beat all the Prince's horse. God made them as stubble to our swords. We charged their regiments of foot with our horse, and routed all we charged."

2. WAR AT SEA

On pages 139–142 we have described ships and their armament in the fifteenth, sixteenth and seventeenth centuries. This section tells how navies were developed and managed. Navies, as well as armies, grew in size during the sixteenth and seventeenth centuries. England became the leading naval power and by 1588 Elizabeth had the most powerful navy in Europe. Other countries, in particular France, Holland and Spain, developed their navies, but at the end of the seventeenth century, England still owned one-third of the world's fighting ships!

The English Navy

You have learned already how fortifications on land were reduced in height, largely as a result of improved firearms. A similar change took place in the design of ships and England owed much to John Hawkins. Formerly, ships had towering castles at bow and stern, but Hawkins wanted these reduced. He wanted the galleons to be slender in shape and more guns to be mounted on them so that they became fast, manoeuvrable gun batteries. Hawkins put his ideas into practice for ten years during Elizabeth's reign, and as a

Elizabeth at Tilbury

result the English depended more on broadsides for their victories than on boarding parties. By the time the Armada attacked in 1588, the English ships could outsail, outmanoeuvre and outgun the Spanish.

One unexpected feature of the fifteen years after the defeat of the Armada was the revival of, not the end of, the Spanish Navy. During these years more treasure arrived in Spain from the New World than in any other fifteen years in Spanish history, some indication that the English Sea Dogs did not rule the sea.

Henry Grace à Dieu

A galleon

The Art of War

Towards the end of the reign of James I the Venetian ambassador reported that, "...for the sixteen years he has been King of England they have never knocked a nail into any of the Royal ships, nor so much as thought of such things". As the navy decayed, piracy increased and by the time of the Civil War the English navy was in a poor state.

The English navy was strengthened between 1649 and 1660 by the reforms of Robert Blake. During this period the strong Dutch fleet was beaten. Blake's victories were due to his courage, and also to his complete overhaul of naval organisation. He issued a disciplinary code known as the Articles of War which, although severe, improved the commander's control of a fleet. Later the Permanent Fighting Instructions were issued. Number 3 read: "As soon as they shall see the General engage . . . each squadron shall take the best advantage they can with the enemy next unto them, and in order thereunto all the ships of every squadron shall endeavour to keep in a line with the chief." At the battle of the Gubbard the English fleet carried out this controlled sort of action. They sailed in line ahead, and this action started a more orderly type of naval warfare, which became common in the next two hundred years.

The line of battle of the English navy was made up of three squadrons. Each squadron had its own flag officers—a vice-admiral in the van, the admiral in the centre and the rear-admiral in the rear. The squadrons were known as **White, Red and Blue**, the Red Squadron being under the command of the Admiral of the Fleet.

The navy under Blake was an attacking force and the cavalier historian Clarendon truthfully said that "he was the first that drew the copy of naval courage, and bold and resolute achievement".

The part the navy played in the extension of our possessions overseas, and the increase in our foreign trade is outlined in other parts of this book.

Monarchs realised the importance of a navy, and foremost among them was Peter the Great of Russia. His ambitions could only be achieved with a fleet and his use of galley fleets on a large scale was novel and successful. On the other hand the continued activity of pirates shows that governments did not have full control of affairs at sea.

The Arts

Descent from the Cross, Giotto

Our Lady of Vladimir, Rublev

PAINTING AND SCULPTURE IN THE RENAISSANCE

The Renaissance was a unique period in the history of painting and sculpture. A very important figure in the development of Italian painting was Giotto. If you compare Giotto's picture, *Lamentation over Christ*, with the picture by a Byzantine artist of the *Madonna and Child*, you will see how Giotto has shown real grief over the death of Christ, by the expressions and attitudes of his figures. The other picture is typical of many Byzantine paintings which kept to a rigid tradition. Giotto broke away from these traditional ways of painting and laid the foundation for the marvellous outburst of artistic activity in the towns of Italy, particularly in Florence and Venice.

You will appreciate the works of these Renaissance artists if you are prepared to spend some time looking at, and thinking about, their works. The illustrations in the following pages and the extracts from

artists' notebooks should give you an idea not only of how a piece of sculpture or a painting came into being, but also an idea of the views these artists held on the world around them. No better advice has been given than that of the art historian Bernard Berenson, who urged people "to look, and look and look till we live the painting".

Virgin and Child, Martini ▲

Madonna and Child, Tiepolo ▶

Virgin Mary of the Grand Duke, Raphael ▼

The Last Supper ▲

Study of drapery ▶

Leonardo da Vinci, 1452–1519

When you have read these extracts from Leonardo's notebooks, write your own brief guide to the art of painting.

"Painting extends over all the ten functions of the eye that is, darkness, light, body, colour, shape, location, remoteness, nearness, motion and rest."

"Among objects of equal size that which is most remote from the eye will look smallest."

Courtyard of a foundry ▼

Lady with Weasel ►

". . . When you walk by a ploughed field look at the straight furrows which come down with their ends to the path where you are walking, and you will see that each pair of furrows will look as though they tried to get nearer and meet at the (other) end. . . ."

"Of several bodies, all equally large and equally distant, that which is most brightly illuminated will appear to the eye nearest and largest."

157

"Remember to be very careful in giving your figure limbs that they should appear to be in proportion to the size of the body and agree with the age. Thus a youth has limbs that are not very muscular nor strongly veined, and the surface is delicate and round and tender in colour. In man the limbs are sinewy and muscular; while in old men the surface is wrinkled, rugged and knotty and the veins very prominent."

"Black garments make the flesh tints of the representation of human beings whiter than they are, and white garments make the flesh tints dark. . . ."

◀ *Studies of St. George and the dragon*

◀ *Sketches for the Sforza statue*

". . . experiment should be made many times so that no accident may occur to hinder or falsify this proof. . . ."

"But if you are on the side whence the wind is blowing you will see the trees looking much lighter than you would see them on the other side; and this is due to the fact that the wind turns up the reverse side of the leaves which in all trees is much whiter than the upper side. . . ."

158

Michelangelo, 1457–1564

The following extracts from Michelangelo's letters and from the works of fellow artists or later writers should give an insight into the work of the sculptors.

▲ *The back view of Giorno*

Moses ►

A definition of sculpture by Michelangelo

"Sculpture I call only that which is produced by means of taking away. Anything done by means of adding on is similar to painting."

Vasari refers to the preparations the artist took in this passage:

"I know that shortly before his death Michelangelo burned a great number of his drawings, models and cartoons so that none might see how hard he had worked and in which ways he had tried out his genius."

159

▲ *Il Crepuscolo*

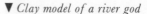

▼ *Clay model of a river god*

Giovanni Battista Armeninni described Michelangelo's method of using wax or clay models.

The Holy family

Stages in the production of a piece of sculpture

"For all his works Michelangelo always made models, but he rectified (his drawings after them) from nature while he proceeded with his work."

Another writer says: "For each full scale model which Michelangelo made there were at least two small models. The first was only a slight sketch, which, combined with drawings showing the measurements of the planned sculpture, served as a guide to determine the right size of the marble block to be used for the work."

On 9th April, 1521, Michelangelo wrote, "I received from Cardinal Medici a letter, and from him through Domenico Buosegni 200 ducats, in order that I should go to Carrara and make there contracts for the quarrying of marble blocks for the Medici tombs which are to be erected in the Sagrestia Nuova of San Lorenzo. I went to Carrara and remained there for twenty days, taking measurements in clay (i.e. clay models) and drawing them on paper."

Vasari described these small models in the next extract. If they were made of wax they could be dipped in hot water and bent as required.

"When sculptors wish to work on a marble statue they usually make first what they call a 'model' for it, which is a guide-pattern, about half a braccio high, a little under thirty cm, sometimes less or more, just as it suits them; and they make it in clay, or wax, or stucco.[1] Such a model shows, in accordance with the dimensions of the block quarried for the statue, the attitude and the proportions of the figure."

Full scale models were used as well. Vasari wrote: "In order that this large model should support itself and not crack, the artist must mix cloth frayings or horse hair with the clay; and this will make the clay tough and not liable to split. The armature[2] is made of wood with pressed threads of hemp or hay tied to it to give the clay a good hold."

Benvenuto Cellini described Michelangelo's method of cutting the block of marble:

"The best method I ever saw was that which Michelangelo used, which is to draw the front view and then carve it round as if you wanted to make a relief, and then to cut deeper and more freely."

[1] Stucco—plaster or cement used for coating surfaces of walls.
[2] Armature—the central core.

MUSIC

Habit de Musicien,

A Musician's Costume

Instrumentalists had been used before the Renaissance, mainly to accompany singers. After 1400 a change took place and they played more as performers in their own right. The church had been the chief patron of music before this time, and was uncertain about, or hostile to, musical instruments being used on too grand a scale. The organ won its place in churches because of its power and capacity for sustained tone, but the church greatly valued the choirs of the time. Choirs were usually made up of boys, with a few men to help, and numbered about fifteen voices.

L

A Group of sixteenth century Musicians

This size of choir was best suited to achieve clarity, balance and restraint. A performance which had these features would have avoided the possibility of a listener reflecting, as St. Augustine did years before, that:

"When it happens that I am moved more by the music than by the words which it accompanies, I confess that I am guilty of a grave sin."

Unlike St. Augustine, Luther was wholehearted in his enthusiasm for music.

162

He wrote:

"St. Augustine was troubled in conscience whenever he caught himself delighting in music, which he took to be sinful. He was a choice spirit, and were he living today would agree with us. I have no use for cranks who despise music, because it is a gift of God. Music drives away the Devil and makes people gay: they forget thereby all wrath, unchastity, arrogance and the like."

Stirring hymns were written and one, *God is our Refuge*, became the battle-cry of the Protestant Church. Luther's greatest change in worship was to give the congregation a much greater part to play in the service, and to allow them to sing and to enjoy the full emotional impact of voices and instruments. To those who were suspicious of music in church he said:

"He who dares not find this an inexpressible miracle of the Lord is truly a clod and is not worthy to be considered a man."

In England the dissolution of the monasteries led to many choirs being broken up and the prospect for music seemed bleak. This was a blessing in disguise, however, for it enabled many choristers to sing to wider audiences than those in the seclusion of the monasteries. One of the great composers of the sixteenth century was Thomas Tallis and he composed as readily in English as in Latin.

In the reign of Elizabeth music gained a status among the arts that it has never held since. There was music for all occasions and foremost among the composers were Thomas Morley (1557–1605), Orlando Gibbons (1583–1615), John Dowland (1563–1626), and William Byrd (1543–1623). The so-called English madrigal, a contrapuntal composition in which each singer contributes to the web of sound, was Italian in origin. The English were willing to use ideas from abroad, but Dowland was typically Elizabethan in the remarks he made about music on the continent.

He said: "The English do carol, the French sing, the Spaniards weep, the Italians caper with their voices, but others bark, but the Germans (which I am ashamed to utter) do howl like wolves."

The Baroque period of music begins in the early seventeenth century and it was the aim of musicians and composers to appeal to the heart. The typical orchestra changed completely by the mid-seventeenth century as these details of the Berlin Court Orchestra show. In 1582, 85 per cent of the orchestra was made up of wind instruments. In 1667 it comprised twenty-one stringed instruments, and one, recently bought, wind instrument. The different wood-wind instruments did not blend into a whole as the string family will. This difference shows the contrast between Renaissance and Baroque music. The former favoured the contrast of sounds while the latter preferred a dominating sound which could be provided by the strings.

Government

Louis XIV

The increase in central power was the most striking change in the government of many European countries between the Renaissance and the beginning of the eighteenth century. Before this time, countries were not so united as modern states are. For instance, the northern border counties of England were often a nuisance to the government in London. England had suffered from the Wars of the Roses when Yorkists and Lancastrians fought for control of the kingdom. With the establishment of the first Tudor monarch, Henry VII, England gained what she had lacked—settled and effective government. National needs became matters of importance in local life. This was partly so because the central government made local government serve its ends. The Tudor monarchs made use of the Justices of the Peace for a variety of jobs such as poor relief, and so made sure that their rule reached to all parts of their kingdom. A similar increase in central power took place in France and Spain. Austria and Prussia showed the same increase in central power, even though Germany was no more than a collection of states at this period.

The best example of central control was in France during the reign of Louis XIV (1643–1715). The remark "L'état c'est Moi", I am the state, which is often attributed to Louis XIV sounds frivolous and a little boastful. However, his ability and hard work during his reign made him the mainspring of progress. Voltaire, the eighteenth-century writer, argued that "It is certain that the love of such glory inspired Louis XIV at the time of his taking the government into his own hands, in his desire to improve his kingdom, beautify his court and perfect the arts".

Monarchs increased their control of the military, religious and economic activities of their countries. Many European states in the seventeenth century had professional armies. Frederick William, the Great Elector, laid the foundation of the Prussian army, whilst Louis XIV's army was over 100 000 strong, even in some peacetime years. Spain and the Dutch Republic fell behind other nations in the size of their armed forces and became less important. The English feared a standing army which could be a threat to their liberties. James II attempted to maintain a large standing army after the Monmouth rebellion. He was forced to flee in 1688 and afterwards Parliament insisted that English kings could only keep a standing army in peacetime with their consent.

The Reformation was closely associated with the rise of a strong English monarchy. Henry VIII's break with the Papacy led to the king denying responsibility to anyone other than God himself. The Stuart monarchs held firmly to their belief in the Divine Right of Kings, maintaining that they were responsible to God and not to Parliament for their actions. These points of view were steps on the way to kings declaring that they should exercise complete control over national affairs.

In economic development and home and overseas trade, the central government played a much bigger part. In England chartered companies such as the East India Company had a monopoly of large areas of trade. Furthermore in the seventeenth century Navigation Laws were passed so as to link colonial trade to the mother country. The three wars between the Dutch and the English in the seventeenth century, (1651–54; 1665–67; 1672–74), were largely caused by trade rivalry. Similarly the Dutch and French set up large overseas trading companies. These companies were the means by which European countries increased their share of international trade. In most countries governments took an intense interest in the development of industry at home. France provides an excellent example. Louis XIV's minister Colbert carried through many schemes which advanced the economic development of France.

GOVERNMENT IN ENGLAND

In Henry VII's reign government was in the hands of the king and a small group of chosen councillors. These chosen few consulted with the king frequently. Henry began the Tudor practice of relying upon men other than the great nobles for advice. This was astute, for Henry could rely on the support of the old nobility, who out of envy and hatred, would welcome the dismissal of men they took to be upstarts. These "new men" proved their value in Tudor times, and included Thomas Wolsey, Thomas Cromwell and William Cecil.

Henry VII called Parliament together sometimes. There were ten sessions between 1485 and 1497, each of which lasted about six weeks. In the remaining years of his reign Parliament was only called once. It appears that Henry needed their support at the start of his reign, but once secure he no longer needed them.

Parliament was used by Henry VIII in a similar way during the years 1529–34. He needed the support of Parliament for the annulment of his marriage with Catherine of Aragon and for the break with Rome. There was little opposition to the king's wishes, partly because of the ruthlessness and skill of the king and Thomas Cromwell, his chief councillor, and partly because many members genuinely agreed with the king's policy.

Royal extravagance was another reason

The House of Commons in 1625

why monarchs were forced to depend on Parliament. Henry VIII had difficulty in getting his early parliaments of 1512–15 to foot the bill for his foreign wars. Later in his reign even the sale of monastic lands and the debasement of the coinage did not bring in sufficient to meet the king's needs. The care with which Elizabeth and her ministers managed the country's resources meant that it was left for the Stuart kings to bring the problem of raising enough money for national needs into an open conflict. Before we consider this conflict between king and parliament we must trace how government developed in the reign of Elizabeth.

Although Elizabeth said in 1569 that after calling three parliaments in eleven years she would not summon another, she did nevertheless call six more. She did this not just to raise money, but because she realised that the nation valued its institutions and would resent the Queen excluding Parliament from the business of government. Elizabeth gave the English monarchy an authority and influence which it had not had before. She did not achieve this success at the expense of Parliament.

The right of Parliament to vote taxes, to make laws and, on occasion, to air grievances was firmly established in Elizabeth's reign, so Parliament increased its stature. The monarch was still expected to live on his or her own income in Tudor times, except in exceptional circumstances, such as war. The rise in prices in the sixteenth century hit the royal family in the same way as other landowners, and with war expenses as well, Elizabeth was £400,000 in debt at the end of her reign.

Economic and social regulations, such as the Statute of Artificers, laid considerable duties on the Justices of the Peace, who, according to Sir Thomas Overbury, spoke the "statutes and husbandry well enough to make his neighbours think him a wise man . . .". These men were usually nominated by the crown, though in some boroughs they were elected. They had to make regular reports to the government of what took place in their district. They were indispensable to the Tudor monarchs for ensuring local observance of the law. The early Stuarts increased the effectiveness of measures such as the Elizabethan Poor Law and their record of local government is good, in sharp contrast with the conflict between king and parliament which bedevilled central government.

The Table of Statutes and the duties laid on J.P.s shows how important they were in the execution of the law.

Parliament

With the crowning of James VI of Scotland as James I of England the two countries, so often hostile to one another in the previous century, were brought together. James believed that the king's authority should be complete and not be questioned, for this authority came from God. This belief in the "Divine Right of Kings" led him to regard the English Parliament with suspicion. It was not their business, in his eyes, to be critical of his policy but to be the servants of his wishes.

Unfortunately James was not in a good position to put this idea into practice. He had to obtain money with the consent of Parliament and if his policy was counter to their wishes, they would either consent grudgingly or refuse his requests. The king was driven to find other means of raising money and such measures as the increase in duties on wine and merchandise led to widespread disapproval. Parliament termed these measures "imposition". Their opposition reached a peak in 1621, and only when James accepted some of their views did king and Parliament work together in uneasy harmony.

The reign of Charles I not only ended this harmony, but led to civil war between king and Parliament. The events leading to the Civil War can be found in the main text; our task here is to see how the quarrel fits into the picture we have already drawn of the development of government since Henry VII. Since that time the policy of the central government depended upon local J.P.s to put it into practice. These were often members of the gentry—the class below the nobility. Possibly Charles failed to realise that the government of his country was like an iceberg with the important, larger part beneath the surface. He was lost without its support, yet he claimed the right to direct its affairs. The opposition to the king wanted effective power transferred from the king to Parliament, they did not want the removal of the king. From their point of view they were out to make the constitution conform to practice. They wanted to end Charles's attempt to rule without Parliament. Charles governed without calling Parliament from 1629 to 1640. England was governed without a monarch for the eleven years after his execution.

Government

Death Warrant of Charles I

New ideas on Government

The period between the end of the Civil Wars and the Restoration was one of political debate and experiment, some details of which we include. So you can try to work out the good and bad points of English government at this time.

The Civil War provoked much political debate. In the army the Levellers had the following programme of changes:

1. Parliament existed to represent the people, and was responsible to the people.
2. Every man, rich or poor, had a right to vote.
3. There should not be a property qualification for voting.
4. There should be a written English constitution which guaranteed individual rights.
5. The constitution should fix the limits of Parliament's power.

The Diggers had ideas similar to modern communists, and they tried to put them into practice in small farming communities. They believed in holding land in common and sharing the fruits of their labour. As one pamphlet ran: ". . . the earth is free for every son and daughter of mankind to live free upon". Private property was to them the source of greed and bloodshed. The ideas of the Levellers and Diggers were not accepted by the Army or by Parliament, but they give us a glimpse of what people other than king and Parliament thought about politics.

The Restoration

The return of Charles II marked the beginning of constitutional monarchy. We mean by this term that the king played a limited part in the government of the country, ruling with Parliament, rather than ruling over Parliament. Charles was voted the customs and excise on ale, beer, tea and coffee and other traditional sources of income which together gave him £1,200,000 a year. The king did not often receive all of this sum as the yield of the duties was lower than expected. Even if the full sum had been realised it would not have met the king's expenses. His debts led him to accept money from Louis XIV in return for help in forwarding some of the French king's schemes in Europe.

An exchange of insults in the second half of Charles II's reign gave us the names of the first pair of English political parties. One party supported the king and the Established Church. The other, which opposed the government, was called the Country party. The Country party, led by the Earl of Shaftesbury, did not want a Catholic king and wished to exclude James, the king's brother, from succeeding to the throne. They called the supporters of the government "Tories" which meant Irish robbers. This implied that the king's supporters were Catholics and criminals. In reply Shaftesbury's supporters were called "Whigs" by their opponents— a Whig being a Scottish outlaw. These parties had very little in common with the

William of Orange landing at Tor Bay

present-day Conservative and Labour parties. It would be difficult to imagine many M.P.s changing sides today, but this was not at all uncommon in the seventeenth century. Men voted according to their own interests so long as they did not create a national political disaster. George Savile, who became Viscount Halifax, was dubbed "The Trimmer". He explained this term in a pamphlet. He said,

"This innocent term Trimmer signifieth no more than this, that if men are together in a boat and one part of the company would weigh down on one side, and another would make it lean as much to the contrary, it happeneth there is a third opinion of those who conceive it would do as well if the boat went even, without endangering the passengers."

The Glorious Revolution

James II had the good fortune to have events play into his hands at the start of his reign. The Monmouth Rebellion gave him a good excuse for keeping a strong army and navy. With such forces at his command he could increase his power and begin to turn the country once again towards the Catholic faith. His policy failed, for England did not want a despotic or a Catholic king. It was a measure of his unpopularity that Whigs and Tories combined to invite William of Orange to be king in his place.

James II's reign illustrated all the dangers that threatened a country if it chanced to have a king who tried to put the Divine Right into full effect. The reign of William III brought a series of agreements between monarch and Parliament which led to a more efficient and freer form of government than ever before. France, despite the glories of Louis XIV, was to take the downhill path to the French Revolution. Our country with good common sense learned from successes and mistakes in government and by 1714 had a system good enough to be the envy of foreign commentators later in the eighteenth century.

The details of the Glorious Revolution can be found on pages 93 and 94.

Let us repeat, to end this section, the main results of this event.

1. The monarch should not be a Catholic nor marry a Catholic.
2. The monarch was granted money for normal expenses once a year. This measure ensured that Parliament had to meet at least once a year.
3. The monarch could no longer keep a standing army in peacetime without the consent of Parliament.
4. The Toleration Act allowed freedom of worship to all except Catholics and Unitarians.

Ideas

The Renaissance

The Renaissance was the start of the most important period in Western thought since the time when civilisation flourished in Ancient Greece. Once more, emphasis was laid on the development of the individual, and in the cities of Italy scholars, writers and artists held a place in public esteem which today is held by outstanding sportsmen and entertainers. The thinkers of Ancient Greece and Renaissance Italy worked in different circumstances. For instance, the Greeks did not have to contend with a dead weight of traditional ideas inherited from the Middle Ages; on the other hand, they did not have the advantage of large numbers of printed books. Only Edison, Marconi and Baird deserve to be placed alongside Gutenberg, the inventor of printing, for only the telephone, wireless and television have enlarged men's powers of communication on a similar scale.

The invention of printing by Gutenberg gave scholars opportunities never enjoyed by people who lived before the Renaissance. A scholar could build up his own library of printed books, the like of which could only have been found in a monastery if he had lived in the Middle Ages. A Cambridge physician left some 200 books when he died in 1551 and this collection contained over forty dealing with medicine.

The Reformation

The spirit of enquiry which grew so rapidly during the Renaissance led to criticism of the Catholic Church. In the eyes of enlightened men, ideas had to be proved in discussion before they were acceptable. Many new ideas, especially in the field of religion, were looked upon as heresies, and it is interesting to note that printing and censorship had the same birthplace, the city of Mainz. The Catholic Church, in the person of Archbishop Berthold von Henneberg, asked that some city councils should suppress dangerous publications. The request led to the cities of Mainz and Frankfurt jointly setting up the first censorship office. In the sixteenth century the Catholic Church issued the Index. This was a list of books which Catholics were forbidden to read.

Title page from Luther's Bible

Many scholars sought the neglected knowledge of the past, whilst printers made this knowledge available to the readers of the period. The ideas of that time, as well as those of the past, appeared in print and had a wide circulation. Luther's criticisms of the Catholic Church were distributed in printed form and, as one historian puts it, "interest in them was general, sudden and unexpected". (G. R. Elton, *Reformation Europe*, 1517–59.) Moreover, Luther's translation of the Bible went through 377 editions by the time of his death and made a considerable contribution to the formation of a single German language. Well might the man who made such things possible, Gutenberg, have an epitaph which read that he was: "well deserving of all nations and languages".

Despite the changes in the Catholic Church, which are called the Counter Reformation, the Protestant movement continued to grow in strength. In Northern Europe this growth went hand in hand with the development of independent national states and almost inevitably strong religious and political differences led to war. Only when such strife was exhausted could some measure of toleration appear.

It would have been much better if the Reformation could have been achieved without the destruction of Christian unity. But to men like Martin Luther there was no going back once they set their feet on the path of Reform. Luther's reply to the charge of heresy, made against him at the Diet of Worms in 1521, has been described as one of "the most momentous events in Modern History". (Lord Acton.) The final part of Luther's reply to the Emperor Charles V who summoned the assembly was:

"Since then Your Majesty and your lordships desire a simple reply, I will answer without horns and without teeth. Unless I am convicted by Scripture and plain reason—I do not accept the authority of popes and councils, for they have contradicted each other—my conscience is captive to the Word of God. I cannot and I will not recant anything, for to go against conscience is neither right nor safe. God help me. Amen." Luther is said to have added the words, "Here I stand, I cannot do otherwise".

You can realise how Luther's words led to the belief that neither prince nor priest should come between a man and his God. As a result many people took the Bible, the written word of God, as their sole guide to life. These people refused to support a state church and despite persecution achieved a powerful position in some countries. The English Puritans, for instance, played a major part in the English Civil War which resulted in the execution of Charles I, so that it looked at one time as though the Divine Right of Kings would be replaced by the Divine Rights of Individuals.

The effect of the Reformation, however, was more to weaken the hold of organised faith, and to lead to a loss of independence by the churches as governmental power increased. Another result, and one which would have horrified Luther, was the growth of economic selfishness. Men who became wealthy and powerful could well argue, if criticised on the grounds that their wealth was based on the misery of others, that they would make their own peace with God. The individualism which was so attractive in a genius such as Leonardo, or admirable in the courageous Luther, was dangerous to the community when it became the narrow self-seeking of a merchant or industrialist.

Lastly we must try to give some idea of how these religious changes affected the people of England and Europe. The scholars wanted the new ideas to reach as many people as possible, and Erasmus expressed this wish in his preface to his *Novum Testamentum* when he wrote:

"The mysteries of kings it may be safer to conceal but Christ wished his mysteries to be published as openly as possible. I wish that even the weakest woman should read the Gospel and the Epistles of Paul. . . ."

Later, Bishop Latimer explained to a congregation at Stamford that it was necessary for him to recite the Lord's Prayer before and after his sermons for so many poor people did not know it. If the old and the new could compromise then there was a chance that violence would not break out, and England was fortunate in the Elizabethan church settlement.

In Europe the seventeenth century brought war, famine and disease in the wake of religious and political dispute and the weakest in the community suffered most. Mutual distrust replaced mutual obligation. The grim experiences of the Thirty Years' War weakened faith and one popular song ran:

> Conscience hither, conscience thither,
> I care for nought but worldly honour,
> Fight not for faith, fight but for gold,
> God can look after the other world.

THE SCIENTIFIC REVOLUTION

You cannot imagine a monarch of the Middle Ages setting down to the work of a mechanic, yet in the seventeenth century Charles II of England collected clocks, fitted up a laboratory and supported the Royal Society, whilst Peter of Russia worked in the Dutch shipyards. Science and technology had become respectable by that time. The renewed study of Greek science in Renaissance Italy led to further scientific discoveries, but there was no sharp break with the science of the past during the Renaissance. This came later with the work of Sir Isaac Newton.

Newton was the supreme figure amongst those who laid the foundation of modern science, just as Shakespeare was the greatest of a remarkable group of dramatists who lived in the Elizabethan age. To be fully appreciated Newton's achievements must be considered against the background of scientific thought before his discoveries were made. The scientific ideas of Greek philosophers such as Aristotle were still studied and accepted in the seventeenth century. Their method had been to solve problems by concentrated thought rather than by experiment.

Seventeenth and Eighteenth Century Microscopes

For instance, Aristotle wrote of natural and non-natural motions. Heavenly bodies moved in circles, whilst stones dropped from a height moved in vertical lines. These were examples of natural motions. Something that was pushed or pulled was moved by non-natural motion, and if the force was withdrawn the body would stop. But how could you explain how a thrown object continued to move after being released? Aristotle argued that air beat on the object and urged it along. Newton was to prove by experiment how bodies would travel for ever if it were not for the force of friction which opposed motion. Moreover he was the first to give a clear

account of universal gravitation.

The oldest of the sciences was astronomy and again it was Newton who gave the complete explanation of the behaviour of the movement of the stars. The system still in existence, despite the work of Copernicus, Kepler and Galileo, was that devised by Ptolemy who lived in Alexandria in the second century A.D. He assumed the earth was at rest and that the stars went through an elaborate system of circular motions. Copernicus suggested the sun as the centre of the system with the earth as a planet but he could not give a satisfactory proof of his idea. Kepler made the next advance by putting forward the idea that the planets moved in elliptical, not circular, orbits. This was a great advance in scientific thought but Kepler still held to the old idea that there was a force which pushed the planets all the time.

In Newton's twenty-third and twenty-fourth years he lived in a solitary stone house at Woolsthorpe near Grantham. These were the years of the Great Plague, and probably the most fruitful years of his life. In his old age he wrote: "In those days I was in the prime of my age for invention, and minded mathematics and philosophy more than at any time since".

Newton's discoveries were in three main fields of scientific enquiry, astronomy, mechanics and optics.

The minutes of the Royal Society for 28th April, 1686, recorded that Mr Isaac Newton had presented a manuscript to the Society. This was possibly the greatest scientific book ever written, the *Principia*.

Voltaire's history, *The Age of Louis XIV*, described this period as a golden age of mathematics and science—an age of enlightenment. The religious divisions brought about by the Reformation were being bridged by what Voltaire called "a republic of letters". In his chapter on the Arts and the Sciences he wrote, "We owe this progress to a few learned men, a few geniuses scattered in small numbers in various parts of Europe, nearly all of them unhonoured for many years and often persecuted; they enlightened and consoled the world when it was devastated by war".

The scientific revolution was to lead to momentous industrial changes in the eighteenth century which gave mankind more power over the world in which it lived than it had ever had before. At the same time the gulf between the educated few and the uneducated mass of the people became greater than it had ever been before, and only today is widespread education making the attempt to lessen the gap between the scholar and the man in the street.

A printer's device: the philosopher under the Tree of Knowledge

INDEX